## *About Llewellyn's Practical Magick Series*

To some people, the idea that "Magick" is *practical* comes as a surprise.

It shouldn't. The entire basis for Magick is to exercise influence over one's environment. While Magick is also, and properly so, concerned with spiritual growth and psychological transformation—even the spiritual life must rest firmly on material foundations.

The material world and the psychic are intertwined, and it is this very fact that establishes the Magickal Link: that the psychic can as easily influence the material as vice versa.

Magick can, and should, be used in one's daily life for better living! each of us has been given Mind and Body, and surely we are under Spiritual obligation to make full usage of these wonderful gifts. Mind and Body work together, and Magick is simply the extension of this interaction into dimensions beyond the limits normally conceived. That's why we commonly talk of the "supernormal" in connection with the domain of Magick.

The Body is alive, and all Life is an expression of the Divine. There is God-power in the Body and in the Earth, just as there is in Mind and Spirit. With Love and Will, we use Mind to link these aspects of Divinity together to bring about change.

With Magick we increase the flow of Divinity in our lives and in the world around us. We add to the beauty of it all—for to work Magick we must work in harmony with the Laws of Nature and of the Psyche. *Magick is the flowering of the Human Potential.*

Practical Magick is concerned with the Craft of Living well and in harmony with Nature, and with the Magick of the Earth, in the things of the Earth, in the seasons and cycles and in the things we make with hand and Mind.

## Other Books by Scott Cunningham

*Cunningham's Encyclopedia of Crystal, Gem and Metal Magic*
*Cunningham's Encyclopedia of Magical Herbs*
*Earth, Air, Fire and Water: More Techniques of Natural Magic*
*Earth Power*
*Hawaiian Religion & Magic*
*Living Wicca: A Further Guide for the Solitary Practitioner*
*The Magic in Food*
*Magical Aromatherapy: The Power of Scent*
*Magical Herbalism*
*The Magical Household* (with David Harrington)
*Spell Crafts: Creating Magical Objects* (with David Harrington)
*The Truth About Herb Magic*
*The Truth About Witchcraft Today*
*Wicca: A Guide for the Solitary Practitioner*

## Video

*Herb Magic*

## Biography

*Whispers of the Moon* (by David Harrington and de Traci Regula)

Llewellyn's Practical Magick Series

# THE COMPLETE BOOK OF

# *Incense, Oils & Brews*

## SCOTT CUNNINGHAM

1998
Llewellyn Publications
St. Paul, Minnesota 55164-0383, U.S.A.

FIRST EDITION
Nineteenth Printing, 1998


Cover design by Maria Mazzara
Interior illustrations by Victoria Poyser-Lisi
Book design by Terry Buske


Library of Congress Cataloging-in-Publication Data
Cunningham, Scott, 1956–1993
    The complete book of incense, oils & brews / by Scott Cunningham.
    p.   cm. — (Llewellyn's practical magick series)
    Revised ed. of: The magic of incense, oils and brews. 1986.
    Includes bibliographical references.
    ISBN 0-87542-128-8
    1. Magic. 2. Incense—Miscellanea. 3. Perfumes—Miscellanea.
4. Essences and essential oils—Miscellanea. I. Cunningham, Scott,
1956-1993. Magic of incense, oils and brews. II. Title. III. Series:
Llewellyn's practical magick series.
BF1623.I52C86    1989
133.4'4—dc20                    89-35510
                                                CIP

Note: The old-fashioned remedies in this book are historical references used for teaching purposes only. The recipes are not for commercial use or profit. The contents are not meant to diagnose, treat, prescribe, or substitute consultation with a licensed healthcare professional.

Llewellyn Publications
A Division of Llewellyn Worldwide, Ltd.
P.O. Box 64383, St. Paul, MN 55164-0383

Printed in the United States of America

For Morgana, *kahuna la'au lapa'au* of Hawaii

# *Acknowledgements*

My thanks go to Marilee and Ed for once again giving me access to their comprehensive herb library, as well as to Marilee for sharing her expertise in incense composition and allowing some of her formulas to be published here.

My especial thanks to fellow author M.V. Devine for allowing me to reprint some oil and incense recipes from her entrancing book *Brujeria: A Study of Mexican-American Folk-Magic.*

I'm also indebted to Ron Garst for his gracious help and willingness to discuss oils and incenses.

Thanks are in order to the many friends, readers and reviewers who gave me ideas toward this revised edition and who compelled me to complete it, and to Carl Weschcke of Llewellyn for presenting the opportunity.

To Annella of The Crystal Cave (Claremont, California), Judy of Eye of the Cat (Long Beach, California) and Karen of Moon Magic (Littleton, Colorado) for assistance in obtaining unusual herbs and oils.

I certainly must express my gratitude to the authors who, in the past, committed some of these secrets to paper so that later generations could reap the rich rewards of working in harmony with the Earth's fragrant treasures.

Finally, I must express my thanks to Morgan (Dorothy), my first teacher, who instructed me in the mysteries of the brews, incenses and oils long before I understood what it was all about.

# Contents

# Preface to the New Edition

Several years ago I began work on a collection of magical perfumery—incenses, oils, sachets and other occult herb products. I decided to include such obscure subjects as inks and ointments in an attempt to broaden public interest in all phases of magical herbalism. I completed the book in 1985; Llewellyn published *The Magic of Incenses, Oils and Brews* the following year.

Even as I sent the book off I realized that much remained to be said on this subject. I continued practicing the arcane arts of herbalism. As my knowledge grew, I knew that a greatly expanded edition of this book was necessary.

Hence, this volume. Most of the original information remains, but in more complete form. Well over 100 new formulas have been included, and most now contain proportions that many readers of the first edition of this book seemed to want.

Every page, every chapter, has been clarified and rewritten. Several new chapters and sections have also been added:

*Chapter Four: Ingredients* is a look at common and rare botanical substances and oils used in creating herbal compounds, together with some recommended substitutions.

*Chapter Five: Creating Your Own Recipes* is a guide to just that—an in-depth discussion with step-by-step instructions.

*Tinctures*—examines the art of capturing plant fragrances with alcohol, a simple and easy alternative to oil extraction.

*Ritual Soaps* details an easy method of creating spell soaps for various magical purposes—without the use of lye or fat.

*Powders* discusses the compounding and unique uses of finely ground herbal blends.

*Part III: Substitutions* replaces Chapter 13 of the last edition. The introduction consists of a lengthy example of proper magical substitution, and the tables have been vastly enlarged. One new feature is a list of specific substitutions: tobacco for nightshade, cedar for sandalwood, for example.

Additionally, a *Glossary* has been added to define various terms; a list of *Sources* of herbs and oils has been included; a *Botanical Index* lists all plants and their Latin names for clarity and a *General Index* completes the major additions to this book.

In manuscript form this edition is nearly twice the size of the last. Though I'm still learning, naturally, I feel that *The Complete Book of Incense, Oils and Brews* can now stand as a comprehensive introduction to the subject.

Though it is meant to be read and used in conjunction with *Magical Herbalism* and *Cunningham's Encyclopedia of Magical Herbs*, it can certainly be used alone.

After all, the greatest teachers are the herbs themselves—words merely echo their lessons. It is to the plants, flowers and trees that we must turn if we would know the secrets of the Earth. Books such as this are signposts to guide the way.

So meet the plants. Bring them into your life and discover their energies. As incense smolders, brews bubble and oils release their fragrances, invite their energies within.

Ritual herbalism is a gift from our long-gone predecessors—an ancient art of touching nature. The secrets await those who wish to discover them.

Scott Cunningham
San Diego, California
October 31, 1987

# *Introduction*

For millenia our ancestors have used herbs to create a vast array of magical substances. Precious ointments secreted within horn containers or crystal jars were rubbed onto the body to effect magical transformations. Brews were sipped or sprinkled to ward off evil and negativity. Fragrant barks and woods were thrown onto hot coals to release their scents and powers.

The actual formulas for such sachets, ointments, brews, incenses and oils were often kept secret, locked within the Witches' spellbooks and magicians' grimoires, or even deeper in the farthest recesses of the human mind. Upon entrance ineo the starlit circles of the "wise ones," these secret recipes were revealed, enabling the student to use them in rite, spell and everyday life.

Today, when the twilight curtains of secrecy are being drawn back so that all may share in the old ways of magic, there is a growing need for a comprehensive, responsible book of magical formulas that will satisfy the needs of those who would mix up the old brews and incenses—not only for magical purposes but also for the sheer joy in so doing.

The composition of incenses, blending of oils, mixing of herbs— such is the work necessary to keep a well-stocked magical pantry. Many delight in putting herbs to work, aligning their powers, mingling energies as they mix leaves and oils; but many more seem to be in the dark about such things.

Hence, this book. Few seem to know how to compound incense— once far more important in magic and religion than oils. And despite public stereotypes of the Witch with cauldron and brew, the art of brew-making seems to be dying out as rapidly as that of ointment composition.

Therefore, this is a guide to little-known methods of magical cookery. The results don't fill our stomachs, but do enrich and better our lives and the lives of those we love.

It should hardly be necessary to say that no cursing or "evil" recipes appear here, as they do in other books.

Also, these recipes are primarily from European magical and Wiccan sources. I have purposely deleted the so-called Voodoo formulas, since they have been covered well in other works (see Bibliography). I have also resisted including recipes that have constantly appeared in print during the last 50 years or so.

Some of the formulas appearing in this volume were passed to me by teachers; others came from old manuscripts, were shared by friends, or evolved themselves as the need arose. Some are indeed ancient, but all will work with proper preparation, empowerment and use.

The best way to become truly intimate with herbs and their magic is to work with them. Let them teach. Compounding incense, oils and brews is one of the easiest and most productive means to learn herb magic.

I have said before that magic must be practical. If you need protection incense at three A.M., you should be able to prepare it yourself. With this book the way is open to you.

Some may find it amusing that, in this day of incredible technology, many are turning to Mother Earth, to herbs and magic. Folks are programming computers to cast spells, etching runes on glowing cathode ray tubes, and waiting for *magic* to dazzle their eyes.

But the keepers of the old ways—the Witches, magis, wizards and wise women—pour scented oils into tubs of warm water, set incense alight and drink brews. They weave spells with herb, gesture and word, utilizing the simple but potent powers resident within the products of nature, directing them with their intent. Power flashes forth; magic is made.

Because herb magic is natural, it requires only those tools of nature. The most potent are the ones included in this book: protection incense, love oil, healing bath. These are the tools with which we can transform our lives and, therefore, ourselves.

May all your transformations be joyous.

# Part I

# Basics

# Warning

Some of these recipes contain dangerous ingredients. Such formulas are marked with the word caution, and an asterisk (*) appears beside each hazardous substance. These herbs (henbane, hellebore, yew, etc.) can be poisonous or fatal if eaten, drunk, rubbed onto broken skin, or inhaled when burned as incense. Caution must be observed in any attempts to use such ingredients.

In fact, it's safer not to utilize them at all. The sale and use of these baneful herbs are mostly restricted by law, so mere possession of many of them can be hazardous.

Recipes containing such herbs have been included here because they are traditional, but sufficient warnings are present so that anyone foolish enough to try a toxic mixture cannot do so unaware of the attendant dangers.

In addition, within the botanical index beginning on page 255, plants have been marked according to their safety. Plants labeled (x) should never be ingested. Plants labeled (~) should be used with caution, since they may adversely affect some people due to their specific health problems (i.e. diabetes, using MAO inhibitors, kidney disease, etc.) Plants labeled (P) should not be used when pregnant or nursing.

Other important cautions:

Oils, incense, bath salts, soaps, tinctures, sachets and powders should never be swallowed. Always dilute essential oils. Keep essential oils out of reach of children. In the event of an overdose, call your poison control center.

Many plants and essential oils are poisonous. All that is knowable about herbs is not yet known, so use herbs and oils with caution and respect. Plants are drugs. Check everything you put into your body with up-to-date herbal reference books.

The information contained within this book is for informational purposes only and is not intended as legal, medical or psychological advice. For help in these matters, consult a lawyer, doctor or psychiatrist.

# 1
# On Magic

MAGIC IS A BYPRODUCT of the oldest science—far older than astronomy, chemistry or biology. This "science" constituted the earliest investigations into nature. What caused the seasons to turn, the sea to rise and fall, the birth and death of all living things?

Magic—the use of natural energies to bring about needed change—arose when those early humans discovered invisible forces around them. Humans were aware of the effects of gravity, electricity and magnetism long before such terms were coined. Nuts fell to the ground. Lightning blasted trees. Animal fur created sparks when stroked on dry days. Metallic rocks strangely attracted bits of iron.

But these early humans discovered more than has been accepted into scientific doctrine. They sensed connections between humans and specific places, between them and the Earth. They intuited forces residing within plants, animals and stones. They felt energies within their own bodies that could be moved according to will and need.

Through centuries of experimentation, error and inspiration, magic was born. It evolved into a tool of personal power, one with a fantastic potential to both help and harm.

The power of magic springs from the Earth itself, as well as from stars and celestial bodies. It resides within winds, rocks and trees; in flames and water and our bodies. Rousing and directing such forces sums up the practice of magic.

Herb magic is a specialized form that utilizes the power of plants. This is the realm of incense, oils, baths, brews and tinctures. An act of herb magic may be as simple as rubbing a scented oil onto a colored candle, setting it in a holder, lighting it and visualizing your magical need.

A more complex ritual may involve several candles, many oils, incense, chants, ritual clothing—all in harmony with your goal. Herb magic can be simple or complex. You're the only one calling the shots.

This is a personal art. It is certainly one in which the practitioner must actually participate. Armchair magicians do not produce results. Those who are willing to dirty their hands and to actually *practice* herb magic are soon improving their lives and themselves.

This book is a compendium of ritual herbal processes and recipes. Though these mixtures contain energies in and of themselves, they are far more effective when used in conjunction with simple rituals.

If you are new to magic you may find yourself asking, "Terrific. So how do I use these things?"

Though directions for use are given in Part II for each type of mixture, a few pages devoted to the basics of magic are perhaps warranted here.


### Harm None

How's that for an opener? This is the basic, unrelenting rule of all magic: *harm no one*. Not yourself, not your enemies, no one.

To me, magic is an act of love, a method of bringing light and order into my life. It is to most other practitioners as well. But not to some.

Many become involved in magic because they see it as a great weapon to use against their nagging bosses, unfaithful friends and mates, and a host of imaginary enemies.

They soon learn the truth.

If you want to control or manipulate people, to bend others to your will, magic isn't for you. If you wish to harm, hurt or even kill others, magic isn't for you. If you want to force a man or a woman to fall in love or jump into the sack with you, magic isn't for you.

Not that there aren't people who attempt such things with magic. They certainly exist . . . for a time. Then, for some reason or another, they quietly fade into the sunset.

Some amateur evil magicians (there really isn't any other kind) think, "Hey! I can hex that guy and nothing will happen to me. I'm too well protected! Ha!"

Perhaps they do have magical protections that will fend off any outside negative forces. However, these magical guards are power-less against the attack that will ultimately kick them off their feet. Where does this "curse" come from? From within.

Practicing harmful magic arouses the darkest, most dangerous aspects of the inner being. No superhero has to throw a curse at the evil magician to right their wrongs. No faery princess need zap him or her with her wand. *Misusers of magic curse themselves.* They do this by unlocking a forceful stream of negative energies from inside them-selves. This is one hex that—sooner or later—never fails to hit home.

So if you're thinking about using magic in this way, think again! You've been warned.

There are subtler misuses of magic. Threatening to curse some-one, or intimating that you're able to perform such an action, violates the "harm none" rule even if you don't intend to perform the action. Harming someone psychologically is as negative as doing so psychi-cally or physically, and will eventually lead the boaster to curse themselves.

Promising a man or a woman to teach them the secrets of magic as a way of getting into their pants is another sure-fire way to lead yourself to ruin.

These are facts, not personal opinions.

The choice is yours.


## Working for Others

A friend of yours is sick. You want to help. Before performing any healing ritual for that friend, it's best to ask them if they want you to. Abide by their wishes.

The same is true for any ritual you may wish to do for some other person. Obtain their permission in advance, even if it's a laughing one. Working positive magic for another person who doesn't want it—or who isn't ready for the results—is manipulative.

So, to make sure that you are truly harming none, ask them before mixing up those herbs.


## The Goal

House protection. Good health. Love. Money. These are magical goals or intents.

The goal is at the heart of all magic. Without a goal, no rituals need be performed. Goals aren't always earthly. Some rites are formed to help the magician tune into spirituality—to Deity, if you will. Others are designed to strengthen psychic awareness (the unconscious mind) or mental alertness (the conscious mind).

When a goal presents itself to a magician, she or he will usually take physical steps to attain it. If these fail, rituals are performed.

Some goals, obviously, can't be accomplished through normal means. When this is the case, magic is immediately used.

### The Power

The power at work in magic is within our bodies as well as within herbs, stones and other natural products of the Earth. It is not satanic, dangerous or evil; nor is it supernatural. Magical power is the power of life itself.

After you exercise for an extended period you're tired. Why? Your body has released a large amount of energy.

A flower dies prematurely after being cut from the ground. It is no longer receiving energy (in the form of nutrients) from the Earth.

This is the energy used in herb magic: personal power and that which resides in plants. By combining these two forces, by moving them from within to without and by giving them purpose and direction, herb magicians create needed changes.

In herb magic—or any form of magic—we must raise and release this energy. There are many methods used to accomplish this. One of the most effective ways is through your emotions.

Why do a magical ritual? Usually, it's because of a need. If you *need* and *want* something badly enough, your personal power is focused toward that purpose. In mixing up an incense, you *mix in* that power. In lighting a candle, you light it *with that power*.

Many rituals are ineffective precisely because the magician wasn't concentrating on the work at hand. Or, she or he simply *needed* something but didn't *want* it. In either case, personal power wasn't properly transferred to the incense, oil or brew, so it was ineffective.

This doesn't mean that herbs and scents aren't powerful on their own. They are. But just as a car refuses to budge without a start, so too do herbal mixtures have to be "started" with personal power to get them moving.

A few pointers here: *Concentrate* on the work you're doing. If

you're grinding rosemary to be used in a healing incense for a friend, *see* that friend in a healthy state. While mixing oils to bring money into your life, concentrate on the oil doing just that.

If you're able to form clear mental pictures, practice *magical visualization* during preparations as well as during the rite itself. See in your mind's eye that the mixture is effective. See it as having already done its work. This moves your personal power into the herbs. In ritual, the energies released by the herbs combine with your own to bring about your magical need.

Magical visualization is the best way to "jump-start" herbal mixtures, but don't worry if you're unable to adequately visualize. Simply concentrate on your needed goal. The herbs will do their work.

### The Altar

The altar is the center of magical practice. It isn't necessarily a religious shrine, though the powers used in magic are at the heart of every religion (a key to unlocking magic, religion and the nature of Deity). The altar is simply any flat area at which you can work with herbs and perform magical rites.

Though magic can, and should be, practiced anywhere as needed (preferably outdoors), indoor magic is best done in one specific place—hence the advisability of creating a permanent altar or working space. This need be nothing more than a coffee table, a cleared dresser top, or a small table placed in an inconspicuous corner. Ideally, it will be in a spot where objects can be left for several days, for some spells must be worked for that length of time.

Though many herb magicians drape their altars with colored cloth, this is unnecessary. So too are fancy altar tools such as expensive censers and gleaming silver candlesticks. A flat, plain space (preferably wooden) is all that is necessary.

If you wish to burn candles on the altar in recognition of higher powers, do so. Ditto for placing flowers as offerings to the gods (or however you view Deity). For best results, magic should be personally satisfying, so create an altar that moves you.

### Timing

In the past, when humans lived in tune with the cycles of nature, much emphasis was placed on magical timing. Love spells (and all constructive rituals) were performed while the Moon was waxing (i.e., from New Moon to Full Moon). Spells involving the destruction of disease, pests and problems were best cast during the waning of the Moon (from Full to New).

Then, too, the hours of the day, days of the week, and even the months and seasons of the year were sometimes taken into account when deciding the most advantageous moment for magical ritual. If the magician was knowledgeable about astrology, the positions of the planets were also perused.

Such complex magical timing was beyond the means of the vast majority of illiterate farming families and common folk who practiced the bulk of natural magic a few centuries ago. If the baby was sick its mother didn't wait two weeks for the correct lunar phase. She cast a spell when it was needed, with the firm knowledge (not belief) that it would help.

Timing is still important to some herb magicians, but I feel that, save for rare situations, its day is past. In magic we work with universal energies that are channelled through our bodies, through herbs and colors. Because they are universal energies, they are universal in origin, scope and influence.

If someone tells me that they can't do a prosperity ritual because the Moon is waning, I tell them that another moon circling another planet is waxing, and that the two balance each other out.

This is the way I see magical timing. But those who feel that it is prerequisite are free to follow the old ways.*

## Tools

The tools of magic can be found around the house, purchased through the mail (see Appendix 2) or easily made. For most herb magic and processing, these few tools should suffice:

- a mortar and pestle (for grinding herbs)
- a large nonmetallic bowl (for mixing)
- a small spoon (for incense)
- a censer (for burning incense)
- eyedroppers (for mixing oils)
- a nonmetallic pan (for brewing)

---

* For more information regarding magical timing, see Scott Cunningham's *Magical Herbalism* (Llewellyn, 1982).

- small funnels (for use with oils)
- self-igniting charcoal blocks (see Appendix 2 or Incense in Part II of this book)
- cheesecloth (for straining brews and tinctures)
- colored cotton cloth and wool yarn (for sachets)
- candles and candle holders
- a large quantity of jars (to store herb products)

## A Basic Spell

We'll use a healing ritual as an example of how magic works. If this spell is for a friend, you've already asked for and received permission from the person to perform the spell.

Take a healing incense, a healing oil, and a purple or blue candle to your altar. Before it, with your mind composed and calm (and the room quiet), light a charcoal block, set it in your censer, and sprinkle a bit of the incense onto the block. As it rises in fragrant, powerful clouds, *will* your mind to focus on your magical goal of healing.

Visualize yourself (or your sick friend) clearly in your mind. Do not see the sickness—visualize perfect health. If thoughts of the sickness enter your mind, banish them immediately; they will only hinder your magic.

Open the oil, and while concentrating on you or your friend, wet two fingers of your right hand with the oil. Holding the candle in your left hand (or right, if you're left-handed), rub the oil onto the candle from the top or wick-end to its center, and then from the base to the center, until the entire candle is covered with a thin, shiny coating of oil.

As you rub it you're sending power into the candle—personal power as well as that resident within the oil. *Feel* the oil's power and your personal power becoming one with the candle. Sense them fusing together with your magically empowered imagination. Visualize!

Now hold the candle, calling upon any powers or deities with which you feel comfortable, asking that they aid in healing the person.

Firmly place the candle in the holder. Add more incense to the censer. Strike a match and light the candle. Watch its flame for a few seconds, still holding your image of perfect health, then leave the area. As you do so, push all thoughts of the ritual completely out of your mind.

Let the candle burn as long as you wish. If you have to leave home, snuff its flame out with your fingers or a snuffer (blowing out candles is seen as an affront to the element of Fire).* Relight the candle upon your return.

This deceptively simple ritual can be repeated for several days in a row or performed once and never again. As you use herb magic you'll discover the number of repetitions necessary for the successful accomplishment of a magical goal.

If you wish, you can greatly complicate this spell. You may stitch a robe of the color corresponding to the spell (purple or blue for healing, green for money; see Appendix 1) and wear this while you perform the rite.

You may involve planetary magic in your ritual. This may mean performing the spell on a Sunday (a great day for healing). Or, you could wear a stone such as amber, which has legendary healing properties. The spell might be preceded with a bath in which a sachet of healing herbs has been steeped.

Since spells often utilize spoken words, invocations or prayers to specific deities can be added, as can chants or magical "words of power," which can be used to direct your energies into the candle.

Then, too, some magicians add music or dance to their spells, or the use of intoxicants (which I don't recommend), strange props, and on and on, with an infinite number of possible alterations to this basic candleburning rite.

How does it work? From the moment you select the incense and oil to be used† to the time you light the candle, you are setting powers into motion. Through your concentration on the goal (in this case, healing) you are sending power, for *concentration is power!*

As you anoint the candle with the energy-packed oil, still visualizing the person (or you) in a healed state, you are sending energy into it from the oil but also from yourself, from the store of personal power that sustains our lives.

The incense smoke sets the atmosphere, sending out showers of healing vibrations, which are absorbed into the candle just as your concentration is absorbed.

Any spoken invocations or prayers to higher beings will also

---

* See Part III of *Earth Power* for more information regarding elemental magic.

† Or, when selecting the ingredients for the incense and oil if you have no appropriate mixtures in stock.

help align your spell with your magical need, and should add energy as well.

As the candle burns, the power you've concentrated within it is slowly released through the agency of flame. Wax is transformed from a solid into a liquid and a gas, a miraculous process in and of itself. At the same time, the energy and power you've poured into the candle is released and speeds on its way.

A spell of this type need not take much more than ten to fifteen minutes once you're comfortable with it. It certainly doesn't require a huge investment in tools and regalia. You'll need a comprehensive stock of herbs, incenses and oils, but that's what this book is all about.

This same basic spell can be used for any magical need. If bills have to be paid, use a green candle, a money oil and incense, and visualize yourself paying the bills: writing checks for them or stamping them "paid in full."

If love is your quest, see yourself with the perfect mate (remember: no one person in particular) as you light the love-type incense.

Magic is not instantaneous, or "snap-crackle-pop," as a friend calls it. You can't snap your fingers or wiggle your nose and expect your life to fall into place overnight. You must back up your magical work with physical exertion.

Certainly all the spells in all the grimoires in the world won't help you find employment if you sit at home all day, never checking the want ads or hitting the streets. The same is true of any type of magic.

Magic is truly an all-involving art. If you're willing to expend psychic energy, you must also be prepared to exert physical energy as well. In doing so, your magical needs will be transformed into solid reality.

# 2
# On Proportions

THE BULK OF the recipes included in the first edition of this book lacked proportions. I explained that herb magic is a personal art and encouraged readers to determine each ingredient's amount.

Many readers who have written to me since the first edition (as well as a few reviewers) have said that they wanted specific proportions in the recipes. So most of the recipes in this revision contain *guidelines* on proportions. Again, these aren't holy writ; they are suggestions.

Many belong to the "cookbook" school of herb magic, in which recipes are strictly followed to produce the finest results, but this isn't necessarily desirable or even possible. While most cooks will have a large stock of such staples as flour, salt, spices, eggs and vegetable oils, many of the ingredients used in magical herb compounds are difficult to obtain, and when available, almost prohibitively expensive.

So the herb magician who insists on using the exact amounts of ingredients for, say, Spirit Incense #6 may end up spending $40 or more to create it. For example, wood aloe currently sells for around $30 a pound—when you can find it. A few years ago it was being sold for around $5.00 *a gram*.

An intuitive (rather than by-the-book) herbalist with just a pinch of wood aloe would add that amount to the product, thereby avoiding a costly purchase for the sole purpose of "accurately" mixing up the incense. Or, she or he may simply substitute another ingredient. (See Part III: Substitutions.)

Feel free to follow these recipes as they are written, but remember that these are suggested proportions. As I said in the first edition:

13

Keep in mind that even if every recipe contained exact proportions, you'd often have to adjust them to compensate for the cup of sandalwood you don't have, the empty rosemary jar in your magical pantry, and the missing phials of tonka and patchouly oil.

If you decide to alter the quantities of recipe ingredients, it is advisable to record your proportions in a small notebook or on three-by-five-inch index cards, to save for future reference.

Don't hesitate to do this, for if you come up with a wonderful oil formula but haven't recorded the proportions, it might take you weeks of testing to duplicate it again—if you ever do succeed.

For instance, when I began practicing herb magic, I mixed up a sachet (which I still have) that smelled indescribably delicious. Being a new student, I ignored my teacher's warnings to record recipes and proportions. (I had invented the mixture on the spot.) After letting it sit for six months, forgotten behind a shelf of herbs, I found it again and attempted to reproduce it—but failed. To this day (19 years later) I still haven't found the secret.

If you decide to create your own formulas (see Chapter 5) or change quantities, take a few seconds to scribble down ingredients and proportions. Don't wait until after you've made the product to do this. It's easy to forget just how many drops of oil or ounces of herb you used. Write down each amount *as you add it* to the mixture.

Another factor that faces us concerns the amount of herb product to make. One ounce, or one pound? Here are some suggestions:

Generally, on your first try with a recipe, keep the amounts small until you've used it and have determined its effectiveness. This avoids making costly mistakes.

*Incense* is usually made up in quantities of one cup or so, since only a small amount is needed for smoldering during rituals. It also keeps well in tightly capped or corked jars. If you wish, once you have perfected the recipes, make up a pound or more so that you have a ready stock on hand.

For cone, stick or block incense, follow the same guidelines—small at first. Once you've perfected the dipping and molding process, it's better to make up large quantities of these items, since they can be messy and time-consuming.

Paper incense is easily made in any amount.

*Oils* are created by mixing true essential oils in a base of ⅛ cup of some vegetable oil. This is a suitable amount for making the first batch.

Once you're satisfied with the blend, make a larger quantity, using the same proportions that you originally used. See why you have to keep records?

*Ointments, brews and tinctures* are usually compounded in one-cup quantities; at least that's how I make them. Only a minute amount of ointment is necessary for anointing purposes, so mixing up much more is needlessly wasteful.

*Brews* won't last for more than a few days before losing their powers (and possibly molding), so they should be prepared in small quantities.

*Tinctures* have lasting properties, but again, only a small amount is needed at any time.

*Ritual soaps* should be in the amounts given in the recipes in that section.

Make up *inks, bath salts, herb baths and powders* in the amounts that you feel you can use. This depends entirely on their frequency of use.

*Herbal charms (sachets)* are simply created when needed. They don't have to be kept in stock.

Keep in mind that in the event of an emergency you can throw together an incense or oil, empower it (see Chapter 3) and use it immediately without recording the amounts. In fact, sometimes I've made up no more than a few teaspoons of incense for a particular use. That's fine—but when time allows, record everything.

When mixing, if it feels comfortable, do it. If you decide to adjust the amounts of ingredients in these recipes, trust yourself. Learn from your mistakes, too, but trust your intuition when compounding mixtures. How much frankincense should be added to the Ritual Full Moon incense, if you decide that my suggested amount is incorrect? Add it until it seems to smell right.

So much for ancient magical rules!

# 3
# *Empowering Rites*

IN MAGICAL HERBALISM we use the powers within plants to manifest needed changes. Herbs do indeed contain energies that we can use to improve our lives.

But these powers aren't enough. We must add *personal power* to the herbs and the mixtures we produce with them. Only by combining plant and human energies will herb magic be truly effective.

Herbs have long been known to possess energies useful for specific needs. Lavender purifies, rosemary draws love, sandalwood heightens spirituality, yarrow increases psychic awareness.

Many herbs, such as rosemary, have several traditional magical uses. A healing incense containing rosemary as its main ingredient should be programmed with strictly healing energies. In effect, this redirects rosemary's love-inducing, purificatory and protective powers toward healing, creating a mixture aligned with your needs. This is done by sending personal power, infused with your magical goal, into the mixture.

This process is known as empowering, charging or enchanting. For this purpose you can use the enchanting procedure described in *Cunningham's Encyclopedia of Magical Herbs* or the following ritual. Neither is more correct. If they don't speak to you, compose your own rite.

No ritual is necessary to infuse herbal mixtures with your power. If you can visualize well, simply touch the herbs (or hold the mixture in a bottle) and send your energy into it. However, ritual is a remarkably effective tool. It allow us to:

• Focus on the magical operation (in this case, empowering)

17

- Build energy within our bodies
- Move energy into the mixture
- Impress upon the conscious mind that the operation has been done, thereby soothing our societally conditioned doubts.

So experiment with various empowering rituals until you find or create the one that produces the most satisfactory results.

## Preparations

Have the completed herb mixture in a jar, bowl or bottle. This empowering ritual is performed with the finished product, not the raw ingredients.

Empower mixtures when you are alone. If others are present in the house, go outside to a quiet spot or shut yourself in a room. Ensure that you won't be interrupted for a few minutes.

Just before the ritual, close your eyes for ten seconds or so and breathe slowly, to relax your conscious mind and to prepare for the coming transference of power.

Open your eyes and begin.

## The Ritual

Light a candle of the color appropriate to the mixture's nature— blue for healing, white for purification, red for love. See Appendix 1 for a list of colors and their magical effects.

Hold the jar, bottle or bowl of mixture in your hands. Sense the nonaligned (i.e., nonspecific) energies it contains.

Visualize yourself with the type of power desired for the mixture. For example, see yourself bursting with health and vitality, or happily in love.

This can be difficult. If you aren't adept at visualization, simply *feel* your magical need. Build up your emotions regarding the mixture's purpose. If you're sick, *feel* the depth of your desire and need to be well.

Now begin to build up your personal power. You might do this by slowly tensing your muscles, working from your feet up. When your whole body is tense, *visualize* (or feel) the power concentrating in your hands.

Next, with the energy tingling in your hands, visualize it streaming into the mixture, perhaps as shimmering strands of purplish white light that pour from your palms and enter the herbs. You may wish to visualize this energy in accordance with the candle's color—blue for healing, for instance.

If you have difficulty imagining this, state in a firm voice your magical intention. For a healing bath mixture you might say something along the lines of:

> *I charge you by the Sun and Moon*
> *To consume disease,*
> *To wash away its causes and to heal.*
> *So mote it be!*

A protective incense may be empowered with such words as these:

> *I charge you by the Sun and Moon*
> *To drive off negativity and evil*
> *Wherever you are consumed by fire.*
> *So mote it be!*

An oil might be empowered to "destroy disease where you are rubbed" or to "spread peace and calm." Again, feel free to compose your own words, suiting them to the mixture and the magical need.

When you feel drained of energy, when you know that it has left your body and entered the mixture, set it down and shake your hands vigorously for a few moments. This cuts off the flow of energy.

Relax your body. Pinch out the candle flame (or snuff it out) and save for use with another empowering ritual of the same type.
The empowerment is done.

This ritual takes little time and can be incredibly powerful. It doesn't require memorizing pages of archaic language or purchasing expensive tools. Once you've become accustomed to the ritual it becomes second nature.

Using herb mixtures that haven't been empowered is one mark of a lazy herbalist. After all, why go to the trouble of creating your own incenses, oils and brews and then omit the final step that energizes and prepares the mixture for ritual use?

Such a ritual, by the way, can be used to charge herb products purchased from occult supply stores.

# 4
# Ingredients

PLANTS, GUMS, RESINS and oils are the tools of the herb magician. These are manifested energies that are available for use in
magic.

It is to the benefit of all who use herbs to learn them as intimately
as they can. It's important that herb magicians know not only which
herbs to use in compounding mixtures but also how to obtain them,
as well as something of their natures.

On a purely physical level, it's vital to be able to identify the best
quality ingredients—the freshest herbs and the finest gums and
resins.

A chapter of this type may not seem necessary to many herb
magicians. "Give us the recipes and forget all this junk," some
might say.

To those I answer, "Fine. Skip this chapter and jump right into
Part II."

Serious herb magicians can continue reading, and in doing so,
learn some of the finer aspects of magical herbalism.

## Obtaining Herbs

There are three main methods of obtaining herbs for use in compounding magical mixtures: collection, growing and purchasing.

## Collection

Walking in the woods, striding through deserts, climbing moun-
tains or strolling along beaches are refreshing activities in and of
themselves. When combined with a quest for magical herbs they can
be exciting adventures.

There are some basic ideas to follow here:

- Collect only what you need. Do you really need five paper sacks full of mugwort?

- Attune with the plant before collecting from it. You may do this by placing your hands around it and feeling its energies, chanting a simple rhyme or a few words that describe why you're taking part of its energy (leaves and flowers), and/or by placing an object of worth in the soil at the base of the plant. If you have nothing else with you, put a coin or dollar bill beneath the plant before harvesting. This represents your willingness to give of yourself in exchange for the plant's sacrifice.

- Never collect more than 25 percent of the plant's growth. If you're collecting roots you must, of course, take the whole plant, so be sure to leave other nearby plants of the same type untouched.

- Don't collect after rain or heavy dew. At least, not until the Sun has dried the plants. Otherwise they might mold while drying.

- Choose your collection site carefully. Never collect plants near highways, roads, stagnant or polluted waters, near factories or military installations.

To dry herbs you've harvested, strip off the leaves or flowers and lay on ceramic, wooden or steel racks in a warm, dry place out of direct sunlight. Or place them in baskets and shake the herbs daily until dry. Store in airtight, labelled jars.*

## Growing

Growing your own herbs is an intriguing art. Herbs can be difficult to successfully grow, but when they do, you're rewarded with a plentiful supply of flowers, leaves, seeds, barks and roots.

Any bookstore or library will have good books outlining the basic steps in growing herbs. Find one and utilize the information in it, taking into account local growing conditions. Most nurseries and department stores stock herb seeds and starter plants.

Magically guard herbs when growing them by placing small quartz crystals in the soil. To ensure that they flourish, wear jade

---

* See *Magical Herbalism* for more information on harvesting and drying herbs.

when watering or tending them, or put a piece of moss-agate in the earth.

When the plant has matured or is large enough, begin harvesting by using the basic system mentioned above. Thank the plant and the Earth for its treasures.

### Purchasing

Many of the ingredients used in herb magic come from far-flung parts of the globe. While I'd love to grow a sandalwood tree on my front porch, it's just not possible.

So, many herbs have to be purchased. This doesn't lessen them in any way; in fact, the herb trade ensures that plant materials which would otherwise be unavailable can be obtained and used in magic.

Mail-order herb and essential oil suppliers are listed in Appendix 2. Send away for their catalogs, and you'll be able to buy magical botanicals from around the world while sipping herb tea in your living room.

Then again, most larger cities and towns have at least one herb shop or health food store which stocks herbs. Check your phone book.

Take care when buying essential oils. If the salesperson says, "Yes, it's *real* jasmine oil!" and it carries a $3.00 price tag, it's real *synthetic* jasmine oil. Even those oils labelled "essential" are usually the products of the laboratory rather than of the fields.

One good yardstick is price. Most true essential oils sell for between $10 and $40 per 1/3 or 1/2 ounce. Some, such as camomile, yarrow, cardamom, neroli, jasmine and rose can be far costlier. Buy carefully!

Synthetics have long been used in magical herbalism, but I urge you to use only true essential oils. (See the Oils section in Part II for more information.)

Regarding herbs: Many stores can't be relied upon to lay in fresh stock at regular intervals, so the rosemary you buy may be several years old. In general, choose dried herbs with bright colors, with few stem pieces and with fresh smells.

Avoid all herbs that are mostly stem, that have varying discoloration, are insect-damaged or moldy. Also avoid any with little scent if the herb is usually heavily fragranced.

Buying by mail complicates this process—it's tough to determine whether the frankincense you've ordered is top quality. Simply avoid ordering more herbs from suppliers who send you lesser-quality botanicals.

And remember—suppliers are at the mercy of the growers. Obtaining a year-round supply of first-grade herbs is often difficult. So use what you can find and hunt for better supplies in the future.

## A Dictionary of Plant Materials Used in Magic

This is an alphabetical listing of some of the herbs, gums and oils found in this book's recipes. A few other substances—such as sulfur—are also included. Additionally, this section discusses plant materials that haven't been mentioned in my previous herb books.

It is designed to introduce you to exotic herbs and oils, with hints on their magical effects. Specific guidelines on selecting the best quality gums and resins are also included. For some of the difficult-to-obtain oils, gums and woods, I've suggested substitutes that can be used in preparing the formulas in this book. (More substitution information can be found in Part III.)

### ACACIA, GUM
(*Acacia senegal*)

Also known as acacia, gum senegal and gum arabic, this is produced by a tree that grows in Northern Africa. The species of acacia which produce gum arabic and gum acacia are so closely related that one product can be substituted for the other. (See Appendix 2 for mail-order sources.) Gum acacia is used in protective and psychic-awareness formulas.

### ALOE, WOOD
(*Aquilaria agallocha*)

Wood aloe, also known as lignaloes, oriental lignaloes, wood aloes and lignum aloes, is a tree native to India. The odor of the wood is described as a combination of ambergris and sandalwood. If this wood is unavailable, try substituting it with the same amount of sandalwood sprinkled with a few drops of synthetic ambergris for incense use.

The last I purchased in San Diego cost, as mentioned previously, about $30 a pound.

Wood aloe is usually used in incenses of protection, consecration, success and prosperity.

## AMBER OIL

True amber oil is created from lesser-quality amber, which is fossilized pine resin millions of years old. It has a camphor-like odor with touches of pine scents, and is rarely available.

Most amber oils on the market today seem to be artificial ambergris mixtures.

It is used in love and healing mixtures.

## AMBERGRIS

This scent, the product of sperm whales, was originally (and rarely) found washed up on beaches. It was heavily used in magical and cosmetic perfumery. Early Arabs used it in cooking. Once the origins of ambergris were discovered, countless whales were killed to collect this precious substance.

It has long been used in aphrodisiac-type oils and perfumes. Its odor is usually described as musty, musky and earthy.

True ambergris is best avoided in these ecologically minded times. Many whale species are nearly extinct. Its exorbitant price is another reason for leaving it to the top perfumery companies to use in compounding perfumes (if it is used at all).

Artificial ambergris or ambergris compounds are widely available, and are usually sold simply as "ambergris."

If you can't find even artificial ambergris oil, try substituting the following bouquet, or compound, which approximates true ambergris:

### AMBERGRIS BOUQUET

Cypress Oil
Patchouly Oil (a few drops)

## ASAFOETIDA
(*Ferula asafoetida*)

This native of Afghanistan and Eastern Iran has a nauseating odor to which the frequent user eventually becomes accustomed, some claim. Even so, I don't keep asafoetida in my home, let alone add it to protective or exorcistic incenses.

If you wish, substitute tobacco, valerian root or any of the herbs listed under these headings (protection, exorcism) in Part III of this book. Rather unbelievably, asafoetida is used in Indian cooking.

## BDELLIUM, GUM
Please see introduction to Part III.

## BERGAMOT MINT OIL
(*Mentha citrata*)
Bergamot is a small plant with a minty-lemony fragrance. It is commonly used in money and prosperity oils. Synthesized versions of this oil abound but should not be used. Instead, make up the bouquet suggested below:

### BERGAMOT MINT BOUQUET
Lemon Oil
Lemongrass Oil
Peppermint Oil

## CAMPHOR
(*Cinnamomum camphora*)
This white, intensely scented crystalline substance is distilled from a tree native to China and Japan.

For many years true camphor wasn't sold in the United States. All "camphor blocks" and mothballs were made of synthetic camphor, which is extremely poisonous.

Quite recently, through the help of a friend, I discovered a commercial source for camphor in San Diego. Camphor currently sells for around $8.00 a pound.

It is added in small amounts to Lunar and chastity-type mixtures.

## CIVET
Real civet is the product of the civet cat, which lives in Sri Lanka, India and Africa. Unlike other animal oils, the animal wasn't usually killed to obtain civet but was painfully scraped.

True civet has an overpowering gamey odor, which is highly offensive to the nose. In tiny amounts it smells sweet, so it has been used in nearly every high-priced perfume.

Today, artificial civet is widely available, and is fine for use in magical oils designed to attract love and passion.

Again, as with all animal products, I don't recommend using the actual substance. The synthetics and compounds that duplicate their aromas are preferred to the genuine and expensive substances. Avoid using all animal products in herb magic!

## COPAL
*(Bursera spp.)*

Copal is a white, pale yellow or yellowish orange gum resin. When smoldered on charcoal it produces a rich, delicious, piney-lemony fragrance. Copal is the North American equivalent of frankincense. While it lacks some of the latter's bittersweet odor, it is a fine substitute for the famous gum resin. When frankincense is left smoldering on charcoal for some time, it eventually emits a very bitter scent. Copal's odor, however, never varies as it burns.

It is native to Mexico and Central America, and has been used as incense in religious and magical ceremonies for untold hundreds of years, beginning perhaps with the Mayans or even prior to the days of that fabled people.

Copal is my favorite gum resin. Frequent trips to Tijuana (I live about 20 miles from the border) have yielded a wide range of copal, varying greatly in price, appearance, scent and quality. The finest copal is a pale to dark yellow color with an intense resinous-citrus odor. It is usually sold in large chunks and may contain leaf fragments.

It is excellent used in all protection, purification and exorcism incenses. It is also effective when burned to promote spirituality.

Copal makes a fine if rather sticky tincture (see Part II: Tinctures). Most of the copal sold in the United States is grown on plantations in the Phillipines.

## EUPHORBIUM

Please see the introduction to Part III.

## LOTUS OIL

There are no genuine lotus oils, though such are frequently sold. Perfumers simply haven't found a way to capture the scent of this aquatic plant. All lotus oils are blends of natural essential oils or synthetic substances that strive to duplicate the delicious scent of the lotus.

Lotus oil is used in spirituality, healing and meditation formulas.

Commercial lotus oil can certainly be used where called for. However, if you wish to create your own, try the following recipe:

### LOTUS BOUQUET

Rose
Jasmine
White (or light) Musk
Ylang-Ylang

Mix until the scent is heavy, floral and "warm."

## MAGNOLIA OIL
(*Magnolia spp.*)

Just as with lotus, no genuine magnolia oil exists. Use a compound magnolia oil or compose your own. If possible, have a fresh magnolia flower nearby while mixing the below recipe. Try to capture its haunting fragrance by combining the following oils:

### MAGNOLIA BOUQUET

Neroli Oil
Jasmine Oil
Rose Oil
Sandalwood Oil

Magnolia oil is often used in recipes designed to promote harmony, psychic awareness and peace.

## MASTIC, GUM
(*Pistachia lentiscus*)

This resin can be quite difficult to find (but see Appendix 2 for possible sources). If it is unavailable, try substituting a combination, equal parts, of gum arabic and frankincense.

## MUSK

A famous perfumery substance, musk was extracted from the scent glands of the musk deer, a native of China and the Far East. Though the extraction could be made without killing the deer, the wild animals were usually slaughtered. Thus, high-priced perfumes were made at the expense of life.

Currently, synthetic musks are readily available and have virtually overtaken the major perfumers, who seldom use genuine musk. As with ambergris, civet and all animal products anciently used in magic, genuine musk isn't necessary or even recommended for use.

When selecting a musk, choose one that smells warm, woodsy, gamey and rich.

Musk is generally used in formulas involving courage, sexual attraction and purification.

Herbal musk substitutes include ambrette seeds, spikenard roots, sumbul roots, musk thistle flowers and mimulus flowers.

NEW-MOWN HAY OIL

This is another perfumer's fantasy. To capture the honey-fresh scent of a just-mowed field of hay, try the below recipe:

### NEW-MOWN HAY BOUQUET

Woodruff Oil
Tonka Oil
Lavender Oil
Bergamot Oil
Oakmoss Oil

New-mown hay oil is used to "turn over a new leaf," to attain a fresh perspective on a difficult problem, and especially to break negative habits (such as addictions) and thought patterns.

OAKMOSS
(*Evernia prunastri; E. fururacea*)

Oakmoss is any of several lichens growing on oak and spruce trees in central and southern Europe.

Oakmoss has a warm, slightly spicy odor and is used in money-drawing mixtures. It is most often encountered in recipes in its oil form. It can be imitated with the following compound:

### OAKMOSS BOUQUET

Vetivert Oil
Cinnamon Oil

SANDALWOOD
(*Santalum album*)
Sandalwood is one of the most valuable woods in the world. It has a rich, mysterious scent and is widely used in magical and religious incenses. Heartwood produces the best quality sandalwood. It is a light brown to reddish color with a deep scent. Lower grades, which are white with little scent, aren't recommended for use in magic. Sandalwood is used in protection, exorcism, healing and spirituality formulas. Cedar can be substituted for sandalwood if the true wood can't be found.

STORAX (Also known as "styrax.")
(*Liquidambar orientalis*)
This resin, which originates in a tree growing in southwest Asia Minor, has a resinous floral scent. It has long been used in magical and religious perfumes and incenses.
It is difficult to obtain. Low-priced storax oil, when found, is usually an imitation of the genuine product. Substitute benzoin essential oil for storax. This doesn't duplicate the fragrance, but it can be used in magical formulas. Or, use any of the oil forms of the herbs mentioned under the appropriate heading in Part III: Substitutions.

SULFUR
This is a light yellow mineral that is fairly odorless until burned, upon which it sends up clouds of the familiar rotten-egg scent.
It is used in exorcistic and protective incenses but isn't recommended because of its persistent, nauseating scent.
Substitute any of the exorcistic or protective herbs listed in Part III of this book, or simply use tobacco.

SWEET PEA OIL
(*Lathrys odoratus*)
No genuine sweet pea oil is available. Try creating your own along the lines of the following formula:

SWEET PEA BOUQUET
_____

Neroli
Ylang-Ylang Oil
Jasmine Oil
Benzoin Oil

It is used in love and friendship recipes.

## TONKA
*(Dipteryx odorada; D. spp.)*

Tonka beans are obtained from Eastern Venezuela and Brazil. They have long been used in creating artificial vanilla, which was widely sold in the United States until it was determined that this product was a health hazard.

Tonka beans are used in love and money-attraction sachets. The synthesized oil is also used. Try this substitute instead:

TONKA BOUQUET
_____

Benzoin Oil
a few drops Vanilla tincture (extract)

## TRAGACANTH, GUM
*(Astragalus gummifer; A. spp.)*

Gum tragacanth is used as a binding agent in creating incense cones, blocks, and sticks. It is a white, slightly bitter-smelling powder which originates in Asia Minor. Some herb shops stock gum tragacanth, as do a few mail-order suppliers. It (or gum arabic) is a necessity in the manufacture of all combustible incenses.

## TUBEROSE
*(Polianthes tuberosa)*

A richly scented, intensely sweet white flower native to Mexico. The synthesized oil is used in love-attracting mixtures, but true tuberose essential oil (actually an absolute) is rarely available. Create a useful substitute:

## TUBEROSE BOUQUET

Ylang-Ylang Oil
Rose Oil
Jasmine Oil
Neroli Oil (just a hint)


## YLANG-YLANG
(*Cananga odorata*)

This strange, beautifully scented flower is native to the Phillipines. Ylang-ylang essential oil is used in love formulas. It is available from virtually every mail-order supplier of essential oils and has a delicious scent.

# 5
# *Creating Your Own Recipes*

THIS CHAPTER JUMPS into the future just a bit, but stay with me.

Say you've been working with herb magic, mixing up some of the recipes contained in this book. Once you've made up several mixtures you might grow restless. Though your magical pantry is stocked with incenses, oils, ointments and bath salts, that may not be enough. You want to make your own recipes.

This is to be expected. Experienced cooks usually create new dishes as situations demand. They may also whip up a new culinary creation for the pure enjoyment of so doing. The magical herbalist is often of the same temperament.

If after trying some of these formulas you'd like to make up your own recipes, you might wonder how to do it. In this chapter we'll discuss this process with full examples to make each step in the creation process clear. Though I recommend it, don't feel that you have to utilize this information. You can make one recipe from this book every week and not run out of projects for several years.

However, this chapter explains the basics for those who wish to create their own formulas.

Why bother doing this? Why not! Such mixtures will be yours alone, intimately connected with your personal beliefs and energies. In short, they may be more powerful simply because they're from you. Old recipes and those created by others certainly work, but it's exciting to create your own unique blends and see their results.

Here's one method to do this. Remember, though, to rely on your intuition when determining which ingredients to add, as well as their exact proportions. And have fun.

## THE GOAL

The first step toward creating a new herb mixture is to determine the future product's *magical goal* or intent. You may have a definite need and are creating this substance to address that need. Or, you may simply be making a mixture to use in the future when some problem arises. If so, decide what you want it to do: bring money into your life, ease depression, create new love interests, draw health or power, protection or peace. For demonstration purposes here, let's say you need to make up a new magical protectant.

## THE FORM

Once you've determined its purpose, decide on its *form*—incense, oil, bath salt, bath herbs, tincture, amulet, ointment and so on. Decide this by answering a few questions:

*Which form is best suited to this type of goal?* Obviously, some forms are more suitable to certain magical interests than others. You wouldn't make up a protection incense, for example, if you need to use it at the office or on your way to work. A protective amulet or oil would be more easily utilized.

*Which procedures do I know the best?* It's wise to use those processes that you have worked with in the past when creating your own blends. Better products are almost guaranteed. (I realize this may be premature if you're just starting to work with herbs.)

*Which procedures produce the best results for me?* For instance, if you're partial to incense, and find the combustible types (cones, blocks, sticks) to be less spectacular in creating your needed magical goal, mix a noncombustible incense. If you've found that burning oil-anointed candles produces the most satisfying results, blend an oil. Remember: Though such products do contain energies, it is their ability to put us into the state of *ritual consciousness* (see Glossary) that determines their effectiveness.

*Which forms do I enjoy the most?* If you abhor the thought of carrying a sachet, there's no reason to create one. However, if slipping into an herb-scented tub of warm water gets your powers flowing, you may decide to create a protective bath sachet or bath salt.

## THE HERBS

Next, decide which herbs to use. Check the Magical Goals tables in Part III: Substitutions to find which type of herbs are magically related to your particular magical goal. For our purposes here, say you'll create a preliminary list of *protective herbs*.

Now check your herb stock. Though time-consuming, it's a good idea to maintain lists of your herb magic supplies. Keep a small notebook near your herbs. On one page (or more if necessary) write down all herbs and botanicals. On another page note the oils you have. On still a third, list all processing supplies: cheesecloth, bottles, eyedroppers, cloth, cord and thread, potassium nitrate, alcohol. On a fourth, keep a list of herbs and oils you wish to obtain.

Each time you run out of an herb or oil, make a notation on the fourth page to remind yourself. And remember to update all lists as you lay in new stock.

This may seem to be unnecessary work, but such a book will save you from rummaging through your assorted bottles just to discover what you have.

The most experienced magical herbalist usually has a cluttered herb cabinet, with dozens or hundreds of jars of varying sizes crowded onto shelves and stuffed into corners. Even if they're kept in roughly alphabetical order or divided by type (such as gums, barks, flowers), checking each bottle can be a monumental job.

Back to our plan. Compare your preliminary list against your stock list. If you have several of the herbs mentioned, fine. If not, buy or harvest more.

Or, determine other herbs that could be used in a protection formula. There are a number of ways to do this. Use your intuition. Look in other books. Or consult the planetary and elemental lists in Part III of this work, cross-referencing the various lists.

For example, since protection is a magical act closely related to the Sun and Mars and often utilizes herbs of the element of Fire, check these tables in Part III as well. Below is a list of various types of magical intentions, together with planets and elements that govern these goals:

BANISHING: Saturn, Fire
BEAUTY: Venus, Water
COURAGE: Mars, Fire
DIVINATION: Mercury, Air
EMPLOYMENT: Sun, Jupiter, Earth
ENERGY: Sun, Mars, Fire
EXORCISM: Sun, Fire

FERTILITY: Moon, Earth
FRIENDSHIPS: Venus, Water
HAPPINESS: Venus, Moon, Water
HEALING, HEALTH: Moon, Mars (to burn away disease),
    Fire (ditto), Water
THE HOME: Saturn, Earth, Water
JOY, HAPPINESS: Venus, Water
LOVE: Venus, Water
MONEY, WEALTH: Jupiter, Earth
PEACE: Moon, Venus
POWER: Sun, Mars, Fire
PROTECTION: Sun, Mars, Fire
PSYCHISM: Moon, Water
PURIFICATION: Saturn, Fire, Water
SEX: Mars, Venus, Fire
SLEEP: Moon, Water
SPIRITUALITY: Sun, Moon, Water
SUCCESS: Sun, Fire
TRAVEL: Mercury, Air
WISDOM, INTELLIGENCE: Mercury, Air

Find the planet(s) and element that governs your particular magical need and consult the tables in Part III to enlarge your preliminary list of herbs.

Once again compare this list with your stock list. Cross out any you don't have at the present time. Let's say the following is the corrected and enlarged list of protective herbs that you have in stock:

| | |
|---|---|
| Rosemary | Frankincense |
| Dill | Fennel |
| Rose Geranium | Rue |
| Tarragon | Fern |
| Basil | Cinnamon |
| Orange peel | Garlic |
| Mint | Allspice |
| Pine | Cedar |
| Juniper | |

Now determine which herbs are most favorable to the type of product you've decided to make. Some of these are immediately inappropriate for incense use. Though garlic is a fine protective herb, it's best not to use it in incense formulas. So cross this one off. If necessary, and if you haven't already done so, light a charcoal block (see Incense in Part II), place it in an incense burner, and burn a bit of each of these herbs. Once again, remove those which don't appeal to you from your enlarged preliminary list. Your smaller list of herbs may now now look something like this:

| | |
|---|---|
| Rosemary | Frankincense |
| Basil | Cinnamon |
| Orange peel | Pine |
| Cedar | Juniper |

Eight herbs are left. In a sense, the recipe has formulated itself. After determining the relative amounts of each ingredient, you could mix the above herbs, empower them, and burn as a protective incense.

Or you could create a recipe using only a few of these. Some possible combinations include:

| #1 | #2 | #3 | #4 |
|---|---|---|---|
| Frankincense | Frankincense | Frankincense | Frankincense |
| Cinnamon | Juniper | Pine | Orange peel |
| Juniper | Cedar | Basil | Cinnamon |
| | Pine | | Juniper |

Many others are possible. You'll notice that I've included frankincense in each combination. In general, use at least one gum resin in every recipe. Resins include frankincense, myrrh, benzoin, arabic, mastic, copal and dragon's blood. Even if one of these gums doesn't show up on the substitution lists in Part III, include one for best results in your new incense.

Once you've decided on a formula, copy it down on a three-by-five-inch index card or in your herbal notebook. Even if you think you'll change it later, *copy it down!* Give the blend a name as well.

Now compound the incense, grinding herbs if necessary in your mortar and pestle, mixing and aligning their energies. Then empower and use, or store in a labelled bottle until needed. You've just created a new incense.

This same basic system can be used to formulate nearly any personal recipe for any type of magical product. Those which are dedicated to specific deities, however, are created in a somewhat different manner.

If you wish to invent a formula in honor of a goddess or god, check into mythology to discover which plants (if any) were used in their worship.* These are ritually appropriate.

Or, use the herbs and plants which relate to the deity's basic influences. For example, in the Pele Incense recipe included in this new edition, fiery herbs are used to honor the Hawaiian goddess of volcanoes. Though fiery Hawaiian plants would be ideal, they aren't easily obtainable on the mainland. Therefore, the ones listed are acceptable substitutes.

With these simple steps you can create magical products for an endless variety of uses. Rely on your inner wisdom. Research. Experiment.

And most of all, enjoy the powers of herbs.

---

* A list of such plants can be found in *Wicca: A Guide for the Solitary Practitioner* (Scott Cunningham, Llewellyn, 1988).

Part II

Processing and
Recipes

# *Incense*

INCENSE HAS SMOLDERED on magicians' altars for at least 5,000 years. It was burned in antiquity to mask the odors of sacrificial animals, to carry prayers to the Gods, and to create a pleasing environment for humans to meet with Deity.

Today, when the age of animal sacrifices among most Western magicians is long past, the reasons for incense use are varied. It is burned during magic to promote ritual consciousness, the state of mind necessary to rouse and direct personal energy. This is also achieved through the use of magical tools, by standing before the candle-bewitched altar, and by intoning chants and symbolic words.

When burned prior to magical workings, fragrant smoke also purifies the altar and the surrounding area of negative, disturbing vibrations. Though such a purification isn't usually necessary, it, once again, helps create the appropriate mental state necessary for the successful practice of magic.

Specially formulated incenses are burned to attract specific energies to the magician and to aid her or him in charging personal power with the ritual's goal, eventually creating the necessary change.

Incense, in common with all things, possesses specific vibrations. The magician chooses the incense for magical use with these vibrations in mind. If performing a healing ritual, she or he burns a mixture composed of herbs that promote healing.

When the incense is smoldered in a ritual setting it undergoes a transformation. The vibrations, no longer trapped in their physical form, are released into the environment. Their energies, mixing with those of the magician, speed out to effect the changes necessary to the manifestation of the magical goal.

45

Not all incense formulas included in this book are strictly for magical use. Some are smoldered in thanks or offering to various aspects of Deity, just as juniper was burned to Inanna 5,000 years ago in Sumer. Other blends are designed to enhance Wiccan rituals.

You needn't limit incense use to ritual, but avoid burning healing incense just for the smell, or to freshen up your stale house. Burning magically constructed and empowered incenses when they're not needed is a waste of energy. If you wish to burn a pleasant-smelling incense, compound a household mixture for this purpose.

### The Materials

Incenses are composed of a variety of leaves, flowers, roots, barks, woods, resins, gums and oils. Semiprecious stones may also be added to incenses to lend their energies to the mixture, much as emeralds were once burned in fires by ancient Meso-American peoples.

Out of the literally hundreds of potential incense ingredients, perhaps 14 are most frequently used. Keep a stock of these herbs on hand if you plan to make several incenses. These might include:

| | |
|---|---|
| Frankincense | Pine needles or resin (pitch) |
| Myrrh | Juniper |
| Benzoin | Sandalwood |
| Copal | Cedar |
| Rose petals | Thyme |
| Bay | Basil |
| Cinnamon | Rosemary |

Be aware that many plants (if not all!) smell quite different when being smoldered. Sweet scents turn sour fast.

If you wish, take a large number of dried and finely ground plant substances (flowers, leaves, bark, roots) and drop a small portion of each herb onto a hot charcoal block; then decide whether the scent is pleasing or not. You might make a notation of each botanical and its scent in a special notebook reserved for this purpose or on three-by-five-inch cards. Also note any psychic or other sensations you notice with each burning herb. In this way you'll eventually build up a thorough knowledge of incense materials, which will aid you in your herbal magic.

Do remember that, as surprising at it sounds, scent isn't a factor in magical incense, except very generally: sweet odors are usually used for positive magical goals, while foul scents are used for banishing rituals.

Scent is power. It allows us to slip into ritual consciousness, thereby allowing us to raise power, infuse it with the proper energies, and send it forth toward the magical goal. However, not all magical incenses smell sweet. Some have strong, resinous odors; others, intensely bitter scents. Incenses intended for ritual use are blended to provide the proper energies during magical operations—not to smell pleasing to the human nose.

Don't let this scare you away from incense, however. Most of our associations with "pleasant" and "foul" odors are learned, and our noses aren't as capable of determining various scents as they should be. Retrain your nose to accept exotic scents, and the art of incense burning will become a joy, not something to be tolerated for the sake of magic.

Occult supply stores stock incense intended for use in magic. Many rare blends can be purchased for a few dollars. While these are magically effective, you may wish to make some of your own.

### The Two Forms of Incense

Incense is virtually a necessity in magical practice, but there seems to be a great mystery surrounding its composition. Fortunately with practice, it's surprisingly easy to make incense.

Two types of incense are used in magic: the *combustible* and the *noncombustible*. The former contains potassium nitrate (saltpeter) to aid in burning, while the latter does not. Therefore combustible incense can be burned in the form of bricks, cones, sticks and other shapes, whereas noncombustible incense must be sprinkled onto glowing charcoal blocks to release its fragrance.

Ninety-five percent of the incense used in magic is the noncombustible, raw or granular type. Why? Perhaps because it's easier to make. Herbal magicians are notoriously practical people.

Also, some spells (particularly divinatory or evocational rites; see the Glossary for unfamiliar words) call for billowing clouds of smoke. Since cone, stick and block incense burn at steady rates, such effects are impossible with their use.

The advantages of combustible incense can outweigh its

drawbacks, depending on circumstance. Need to burn some money-drawing incense for an unexpected ritual? You could take out the censer, a charcoal block and the incense, light the charcoal, place it in the censer and sprinkle incense onto it. Or you could pull out a cone of money-drawing incense, light it, set it in the censer and get on with your ritual.

Different magicians prefer different types of incense. I'm partial to raw or noncombustible incenses, but the wise magical herbalist stocks both types. Hence, instructions for the preparation of both forms appear here.


## Noncombustible Incense

Be sure you have all necessary ingredients. If you lack any, decide on substitutions (see Chapter 5 or Part III for ideas).

Each ingredient must be finely ground, preferably to a powder, using either a mortar and pestle or an electric grinder. Some resins won't powder easily, but with practice you'll find the right touch. When I first worked with herbs I couldn't powder frankincense. It kept on gumming to the sides of the mortar and to the tip of the pestle. After a while I stopped fighting it (and cursing it, I'll admit—not a good thing to do with herbs used in incenses) and got into the flow of the work. The frankincense came out just fine.

When all is ready, fix your mind on the incense's goal—protection, love, health. In a large wooden or ceramic bowl, mix the resins and gums together with your hands. While mingling these fragrant substances, also mix their energies. Visualize your personal power—vibrating with your magical goal—exiting your hands and entering the incense. It is this that makes homemade incense more effective than its commercial counterparts.

Next, mix in all the powdered leaves, barks, flowers and roots. As you mix, continue to visualize or concentrate on the incense's goal.

Now add any oils or liquids (wine, honey, etc.) that are included in the recipe. Just a few drops are usually sufficient. On the subject of oils: If there's a sufficient amount of dry ingredients in the recipe, you can substitute an oil for an herb you lack. Simply ensure that the oil is an essential oil, for synthetics smell like burning plastic when smoldered.

Once all has been thoroughly mixed, add any powdered gemstones or other power boosters. A few—not many—of the recipes in this book call for a pinch of powdered stone.

To produce this, simply take a small stone of the required type and pound it in a metal mortar and pestle (or simply smash it with a hammer against a hard surface). Grind the resulting pieces into a powder and add no more than the scantest pinch to the incense.

One general power-boosting "stone" is amber. A pinch of this fossilized resin added to any mixture will increase its effectiveness, but this can be rather expensive.

The incense is now fully compounded. Empower the incense (see Chapter 2) and it is done. Store in a tightly capped jar. Label carefully, including the name of the incense and date of composition. It is ready for use when needed.

## Combustible Incense

Combustible incense (in the form of cones, blocks and sticks) is fairly complex in its composition, but many feel the results are worth the extra work.

To be blunt, this aspect of incense composition isn't easy. Some of the ingredients are difficult to obtain, the procedure tends to be messy and frustrating, and some even question whether combustible incense is as magically effective as its noncombustible counterpart. For years I hesitated making or using sticks, cones or blocks because they contain potassium nitrate. This substance is magically related to Mars, and I felt this might add unneeded aggressive energies to the incense.

But when I considered that the charcoal blocks I use to burn noncombustible incense also contain saltpeter, I relented and experimented. However, to this day I prefer the raw form. To each their own.

At first, making combustible incense may seem impossible to accomplish. But persevere and you'll be rewarded with the satisfaction of lighting incense cones you've made yourself.

Gum tragacanth glue or mucilage is the basic ingredient of all molded incenses. Gum tragacanth is available at some herb stores; at one time in the past every drugstore carried it. It is rather expensive ($3.00 an ounce as of this writing), but a little will last for months.

To make tragacanth glue, place a teaspoon of the ground herb in a glass of warm water. Mix thoroughly until all particles are dispersed. To facilitate this, place in a bowl and whisk or beat with an egg beater. This will cause foam to rise, but it can be easily skimmed off or allowed to disperse. The gum tragacanth has enormous absorption qualities; an ounce will absorb up to one gallon of water in a week.

Let the tragacanth absorb the water until it becomes a thick, bitter-smelling paste. The consistency of the mixture depends on the form of incense desired. For sticks (the most difficult kind to make) the mixture should be relatively thin. For blocks and cones a thicker mucilage should be made. This is where practice comes in handy; after a session or two you will automatically know when the mucilage is at the correct consistency.

If you can't find tragacanth, try using gum arabic in its place. This, too, absorbs water. I haven't tried using it for incense yet, but all reports say it works as well as tragacanth.

When you have made the trag glue, cover with a wet cloth and set aside. It will continue to thicken as it sits, so if it becomes too thick add a bit of water and stir thoroughly.

Next, make up the incense base. Not all formulas in this book can be used for combustible incense; in fact, most of them were designed to be used as noncombustible incenses. Fortunately, by adding the incense to a base it should work well. Here's one standard formula for an incense base:

## CONE INCENSE BASE

6 parts ground Charcoal (*not* self-igniting)
1 part ground Benzoin
2 parts ground Sandalwood
1 part ground Orris root (this "fixes" the scent)
6 drops essential oil (use the oil form of one of the ingredients in the incense)
2 to 4 parts mixed, *empowered* incense

Mix the first four ingredients until all are well blended. Add the drops of essential oil and mix again with your hands. The goal is to create a powdered mixture with a fine texture. If you wish, run the mixture through a grinder or the mortar again until it is satisfactory.

Add two to four parts of the completed and empowered incense mixture (created according to the instructions for Noncombustible

Incense above). Combine this well with your hands.

Then using a small kitchen scale, weigh the completed incense and add ten percent potassium nitrate. If you've made ten ounces of incense, add one ounce potassium nitrate. Mix this until the white powder is thoroughly blended.

Saltpeter should constitute no more than ten percent of the completed bulk of the incense. If any more is added, it will burn too fast; less, and it might not burn at all.

Potassium nitrate isn't difficult to obtain. I buy mine at drug stores, so check these (it isn't usually on the shelf; ask for it at the pharmacy). If you have no luck, try chemical supply stores.

Next, add the tragacanth glue. Do this a teaspoon at a time, mixing with your hands in a large bowl until all ingredients are wetted. For cone incense you'll need a very stiff, dough-like texture. If it is too thick it won't properly form into cones and will take forever to dry. The mixture should mold easily and hold its shape.

On a piece of waxed paper, shape the mixture into basic cone shapes, exactly like the ones you've probably bought. If this form isn't used, the incense might not properly burn.

When you've made up your cone incense, let it dry for two to seven days in a warm place. Your incense is finished.

For *block incense* make a 1/3 inch-thick square of the stiff dough on waxed paper. Cut with a knife into one-inch cubes as if you were cutting small brownies. Separately slightly and let dry.

*Stick incense* can be attempted as well. Add more tragacanth glue to the mixed incense and base until the mixture is wet but still rather thick. The trick here is in determining the proper thickness of the incense/tragacanth mixture and in finding appropriate materials to use. Professional incense manufacturers use thin bamboo splints, which aren't available. So try homemade wooden or bamboo splints, broom straws, very thin twigs, or those long wooden cocktail skewers that are available at some grocery and oriental food stores.

Dip the sticks into the mixture, let them sit upright and then dip again. Several dippings are usually necessary; this is a most difficult process.

When the sticks have accumulated a sufficient amount of the incense, poke them into a slab of clay or some other substance so that they stand upright. Allow them to dry.

One variation on stick incense making uses a stiffer incense dough. Pat down the dough on waxed paper until it is very thin. Place the stick on the dough. Roll a thin coating of dough around the stick. The incense shouldn't be more than twice the thickness of the stick. Squeeze or press it onto the stick so that it will stay put, and let dry.

Personally, I find the inclusion of charcoal in this recipe to be distasteful and unnecessary. It makes it imperative that you wash your hands numerous times throughout this process. Although traditional, charcoal also lends a peculiar odor to the incense. So here's another recipe I've used with good results:

### CONE INCENSE BASE #2

6 parts powdered Sandalwood (or Cedar, Pine, Juniper)
2 parts powdered Benzoin (or Frankincense, Myrrh, etc.)
1 part ground Orris root
6 drops essential oil (use the oil form of one of the incense ingredients)
3 to 5 parts *empowered* incense mixture

In this recipe, powdered wood is used in place of the charcoal. Use sandalwood if it's included in the incense recipe. If not, use cedar, pine or juniper, depending on the type of incense to be made. Try to match the wood base of this incense to the incense's recipe. If you can't, simply use sandalwood.

Mix the first three ingredients until combined. Add the oil and mix again. Then add three to five parts of the completed incense to this. Again, this should be a powder. Weigh and add ten percent potassium nitrate.

Mix, add the gum tragacanth glue, combine again and mold in the methods described above.

### Rules of Combustible Incense Composition

Here are some guidelines to follow when compounding combustible incense. These are for use with the Cone Incense Base #2 recipe above. If they aren't followed, the incense won't properly burn. There's less room for experimentation here than with noncombustible incenses.

First off, *never* use more than ten percent saltpeter. Ever!

Also, keep woods (such as sandalwood, wood aloe, cedar, juniper and pine) and gum resins (frankincense, myrrh, benzoin, copal) in the proper proportions: *at least twice as much powdered wood as resins.* If there's more resinous matter, the mixture won't burn.

Naturally, depending on the type of incense you're adding to the base, you may have to juggle some proportions accordingly. Simply ensure that frankincense and its kin never constitute more than one-third of the final mixture, and all should be well.

Though this hasn't covered all aspects of combustible incense making (that could be a book in itself), it should provide you with enough guidelines to make your own. Experiment, but keep these rules in mind.

### Incense Papers

Incense papers are a delightful variation of combustible incense. Here, rather than using charcoal and gum tragacanth, tinctures and paper are the basic ingredients. When finished you'll have produced several strips of richly scented paper that can be smoldered with a minimum of fuss.

To make incense papers, take a piece of white blotter paper and cut it into six-inch strips about an inch wide.

Next, add one and one-half teaspoons potassium nitrate to one-half cup very warm water. Stir until the saltpeter is completely dissolved.

Soak the paper strips in the saltpeter solution until thoroughly saturated. Hang them up to dry.

You now have paper versions of the charcoal blocks used to burn incense. The obstacle in scenting them is to overcome the normal smell of burning paper. For this reason, heavy fragrances should be used, such as tinctures. (See Tinctures section in this book.)

Tinctures compounded from gums and resins seem to produce the best results. I've tried using true essential oils with incense papers but without much success.

Empower the tincture(s) with your magical need, then pour a few drops of the tincture onto one strip of paper. Smear this over the paper and add more drops until it is completely coated on one side.

Hang the strip up to dry and store in labelled, airtight containers until needed.

To speed drying, turn on the oven to a low temperature, leave the door open, and place the soaked incense papers on the rack. Remove them when dry.

Generally speaking, incense papers should be made with one tincture rather than mixtures. But, once again, try various formulas until you come up with positive results.

To use incense papers, simply remove one paper and hold it above your censer. Light one tip with a match, and after it is completely involved in flame, quickly blow it out. Place the glowing paper in your censer and let it smolder, visualizing or working your magical ritual.

Incense papers should burn slowly and emit a pleasant scent, but again your results will vary according to the strength of the tincture and the type of paper used.

Plain unscented incense papers can be used in place of charcoal blocks. For this purpose soak the papers in the potassium nitrate solution and let dry, then set one alight in the censer. Sprinkle a thin layer of the incense over the paper. As it burns the paper will also smolder your incense.

You may have difficulty in keeping incense paper lit. The secret here is to allow air to circulate below the papers. You can ensure this by either placing the paper on some heat-proof object in the censer, or by filling the censer with salt or sand and thrusting one end of the paper into this, much as you might with incense sticks. The paper should burn all the way to its end.

Incense papers are a simple and enjoyable alternative to normal combustible incense. Try them!


### The Censer

Whether you use raw incense, blocks or incense papers, you'll need an incense burner. The censer can be anything from a gilt, chain-equipped, church-type affair to a bowl of sand or salt. It truly doesn't matter. I know occultists who've used the bowl-and-salt method for years, long after they could have afforded to purchase other censers.

Although I have several, perhaps my favorite censer is actually a mortar from Mexico. It is carved from lava, stands on three legs and is perfect for use as a censer.

Your own taste should determine which censer is right for you. If nothing else is available, use a bowl half-filled with sand or salt and get on with it. The sand protects the bowl and the surface on which it sits against heat. It also provides a handy place on which to prop up stick incense.

## *Using Combustible Incense*

Simply light it, blow out the flame after the tip is glowing, and set it in the censer. As it burns visualize your magical goal manifesting in your life. It's that simple. You may wish to also burn candles of the appropriate color, perhaps anointed with a scented oil that is also aligned with your goal.

Naturally, incense may also be smoldered as a part of a larger ritual.

## *Using Noncombustible Incense*

Light a self-igniting charcoal block (see below) and place it in a censer. Once the block is glowing and saltpeter within it has stopped sparkling, sprinkle a half-teaspoon or so of the incense on the block. Use a small spoon if you wish. It will immediately begin to burn, and in doing so, release fragrant smoke.*

Remember: Use just a small amount of incense at first. When the smoke begins to thin out, add more. If you dump on a spoonful of incense it will probably extinguish the charcoal block, so use small amounts. Incenses containing large amounts of resins and gums (frankincense, myrrh and so on) burn longer than those mainly composed of woods and leaves.

Don't knock off the ash that forms on top of the charcoal unless the incense starts to smell foul. In such a case, scrape off the burning incense and the ash with a spoon and add a fresh batch. Frankincense does tend to smell odd after smoldering for some time.

Incense can be burned as part of a magical ritual, to honor higher forces, or as a direct act of magic, such as to clear a house of negativity and to smooth peaceful vibrations throughout it.

---

* There's a difference between burning and smoldering; though I use such terms as "burn this incense" several times in this book, I really mean "smolder."

### Charcoal Blocks

These are necessities for burning noncombustible incense. They're available in a wide range of sizes, from over an inch in diameter (they're usually round) to about a half-inch size. Most religious and occult supply stores stock them, and they can be obtained from mail-order suppliers (see Appendix 2).

Potassium nitrate is added to these charcoal blocks during their manufacture to help them ignite. When touched with a lit match, fresh charcoal blocks erupt into a sparkling fire which quickly spreads across the block. If you wish, hold the block. It may light easily. If so, quickly place it in the censer to avoid burning your fingers. Or, light the block in the censer itself, thereby preventing burns. This is somewhat harder to do.

Unfortunately, some charcoal blocks aren't fresh, have been exposed to moisture, or haven't been properly saturated with the potassium nitrate solution and so don't light well. If this is the case, relight the block until it is evenly glowing and red. Then pour on the incense.

### Simple Incenses

These are one-herb incenses that can be burned on charcoal when needed. Since they aren't mixtures, I didn't include them in the following alphabetical listing of recipes but placed them here.

In effect they're instant incenses, needing no mixing or measuring. Simply grind and empower them before use.

**Allspice**

Burn to attract money and luck and to provide extra physical energy.

**Arabic, Gum**

Use for purification and protection of the home.

**Bay**

Use a small amount for purification, healing, protection and to sharpen psychic powers.

**Benzoin**

For purification, prosperity and increasing mental powers.

**Cedar**
Smolder for purification, protection, to speed healing and promote spirituality, and to obtain money.

**Cinnamon**
Burn to sharpen psychic powers, to draw money, speed healing, confer protection and to strengthen love.

**Clove**
Protection, exorcism, money, love and purification.

**Copal**
Burn for protection, cleansing, purification, to promote spirituality, and to purify quartz crystals and other stones before use in magic.

**Dragon's Blood**
Use for love, protection, exorcism and sexual potency.

**Fern**
Burn the dried fronds indoors to exorcise evil, and outdoors to bring rain.

**Frankincense**
Protection, exorcism, spirituality, love and consecration.

**Juniper**
Exorcism, protection, healing and love.

**Myrrh**
Healing, protection, exorcism, peace, consecration, meditation.

**Pine**
Smolder for money, purification, healing and exorcism.

**Rosemary**
Burn for protection, exorcism, purification, healing and to cause sleep; to restore or maintain youth, to bring love and to increase intellectual powers.

**Sage**
Smolder to promote healing and spirituality.

**Sandalwood**
For protection, healing, exorcism, spirituality.

**Thyme**
Health, healing, purification.

### Incense Recipes

These recipes, unlike those that appeared in the previous edition of this book, now contain *suggested* proportions. Several new recipes have also been included, and others have in some instances been improved.

Those ingredients which are poisonous, restricted or illegal under current laws in the United States have been marked with an asterisk (*). These herbs aren't recommended! For best results substitute other, less dangerous ingredients for these herbs. Tobacco is always appropriate (see the introduction to Part III).

#### ABRAMELIN INCENSE

2 parts Myrrh
1 part Wood Aloe
a few drops Cinnamon oil

Burn to contact spirits during rituals or as a simple consecration incense to sanctify the altar or magical tools.

#### AIR INCENSE (*caution!*)

4 parts Benzoin
2 parts Gum Mastic
1 part Lavender
1 pinch Wormwood*
1 pinch Mistletoe*

Burn to invoke the powers of the element of Air, or to increase intellectual powers; to obtain travel; for communication, study and concentration, or to end drug addiction. Smolder during divinatory rituals.

#### ALTAR INCENSE

3 parts Frankincense
2 parts Myrrh
1 part Cinnamon

Burn as a general incense on the altar to purify the area.

## APHRODITE INCENSE

1 part Cinnamon
1 part Cedar
a few drops Cypress oil

Burn during rituals designed to attract love.

## APOLLO INCENSE

4 parts Frankincense
2 parts Myrrh
2 parts Cinnamon
1 part Bay

Burn during divination and healing rituals.

## APPARITION INCENSE (*caution!*)

3 parts Wood Aloe
2 parts Coriander
1 part Camphor
1 part Mugwort
1 part Flax
1 part Anise
1 part Cardamom
1 part Chicory
1 part Hemp*

Burn to cause apparitions to appear, if you really want this to happen.

## ARIES INCENSE

2 parts Frankincense
1 part Juniper
3 drops Cedarwood oil

Burn as a personal altar or household incense to increase your own powers.

## ASTRAL TRAVEL INCENSE

3 parts Sandalwood
3 parts Benzoin
1 part Mugwort
1 part Dittany of Crete

Burn a small amount in the room to aid in projecting the astral body.

## AQUARIUS INCENSE

1 part Sandalwood
1 part Cypress
1 part Pine resin

Burn as a personal altar or household incense to increase your own powers.

## BABYLONIAN RITUAL INCENSE

3 parts Cedar
2 parts Juniper
1 part Cypress
1 part Tamarisk

Burn during Babylonian and Sumerian magical rituals, or when attuning with such deities as Inanna, Marduk, Enlil, Tiamat and others.

## BELTANE INCENSE

3 parts Frankincense
2 parts Sandalwood
1 part Woodruff
1 part Rose petals
a few drops Jasmine oil
a few drops Neroli oil

Burn during Wiccan rituals on Beltane (April 30th) or on May Day for fortune and favors and to attune with the changing of the seasons.

### BINDING INCENSE (*caution!*)

4 parts Nettle
4 parts Thistle
4 parts Knotgrass
1/4 part Nightshade*
1/4 part Aconite (Wolfsbane)*

Burn with caution during outdoor rituals to destroy baneful habits and thoughts. Small amounts only. *Do not inhale fumes!*

### BORN AGAIN INCENSE

3 parts Frankincense
1 part Mullein
1 part Mums (Chrysanthemums)

Burn when distraught over the passing of a friend or loved one.

### BUSINESS INCENSE

2 parts Benzoin
1 part Cinnamon
1 part Basil

Burn to attract customers.

### CANCER INCENSE (MOONCHILDREN)

2 parts Myrrh
1 part Sandalwood
1 part Eucalyptus
1 part Lemon peel (or a few drops Lemon oil)

Use as a personal altar or household incense to increase your own powers.

### CAPRICORN INCENSE

2 parts Sandalwood
1 part Benzoin
a few drops Patchouly oil

Use as a personal altar or household incense to increase your own powers.

### CEREMONIAL MAGIC INCENSE

3 parts Frankincense
2 parts Gum Mastic
1 part Wood Aloe

This formula, from the *Key of Solomon* (see Bibliography), is typical of grimoire-type recipes. It can be used in general magical workings to raise power and to purify the area. Other recipes include such ingredients as mace, brandy and vervain.

### CEREMONIAL MAGIC INCENSE #2

2 parts Frankincense
1 part Wood Aloe
a few drops Musk oil
a few drops Ambergris oil

Another like the above.

### CIRCLE INCENSE

4 parts Frankincense
2 parts Myrrh
2 parts Benzoin
1 part Sandalwood
1/2 part Cinnamon
1/2 part Rose petals
1/4 part Vervain
1/4 part Rosemary
1/4 part Bay

Use for general workings in the Circle,* the ritual working space of Wiccans and magicians, and as a general ritual incense.

---

* The Circle is created by directing personal power to form a sphere of energy surrounding the ritual area. See Raymond Buckland's *The Complete Book of Witchcraft* or Scott Cunningham's *Wicca—A Guide for the Solitary Practitioner* for details.

## CLEARING INCENSE

3 parts Frankincense
3 parts Copal
2 parts Myrrh
1 part Sandalwood

Burn this incense to clear your home of negative vibrations, especially when household members are arguing or when the house seems heavy and thick with anger, jealousy, depression, fear and other negative emotions. Leave the windows open while burning this mixture.

## CONSECRATION INCENSE

2 parts Wood Aloe
1 part Mace
1 part Storax (or Gum Arabic)
1 part Benzoin

When purifying or consecrating magical tools, jewelry, quartz crystals and other stones, smolder this incense and pass the tool through its smoke several times. Do this while visualizing the fumes purifying the tool.

## COURAGE INCENSE

2 parts Dragon's Blood
1 part Frankincense
1 part Rose Geranium leaves (or a few drops Rose Geranium oil)
a few drops Tonka bouquet
a few drops Musk oil

Smolder this incense when you lack courage. If you are in a situation where you cannot burn it, recall its scent and be strong. If tonka bouquet is unavailable, use tonka tincture or vanilla tincture (or extract).

### CRYSTAL PURIFICATION INCENSE

2 parts Frankincense
2 parts Copal
1 part Sandalwood
1 part Rosemary
1 pinch finely powdered Salt
1 small, purified Quartz Crystal point

To use, pour a bit of the incense (leaving the crystal in the jar) onto charcoal. Smolder, and pass the crystals to be purified through the smoke, visualizing the smoke wafting away the stone's impurities. Naturally, this incense can be used in conjunction with the other recommended purifying rituals, or in place of them.*

### CURSE-BREAKER INCENSE

2 parts Sandalwood
1 part Bay

Burn at night near an open window if you feel "cursed." Though curses are rare, if we believe we are cursed, we are! Therefore, smolder this incense and visualize it banishing all negativity from you. Repeat this ritual for seven nights during the Waning Moon, if possible or desirable.

### CURSE-BREAKER INCENSE #2

2 parts Sandalwood
1 part Bay
1 part Rosemary

Another like the above.

### CURSE-BREAKER INCENSE # 3

2 parts Frankincense
1 part Rosemary
1 part Dragon's Blood

Smolder to remove negativity in general.

---

* To cleanse the small quartz crystal, leave it in sunlight for a few days, place it in running water overnight, or bury it in the Earth for a week.

### DIVINATION INCENSE (*caution!*)

1 part Clove*
1 part Chicory
1 part Cinquefoil

Smolder during or directly before using tarot cards, magic mirrors, quartz crystal spheres, rune stones and so on. But be aware: this incense doesn't smell great!

### DIVINATION INCENSE # 2

2 parts Sandalwood
1 part Orange peel
1 part Mace
1 part Cinnamon

Another like the above, and this one smells better.

### DREAM INCENSE

2 parts Sandalwood
1 part Rose petals
1 part Camphor
a few drops Tuberose bouquet
a few drops Jasmine oil

Burn a bit in the bedroom prior to sleep to produce psychic dreams. Remove the censer from the room before retiring. Use only genuine camphor (see Chapter 4). If this is unavailable, add a few drops spirits of camphor, which is available in most drug stores.

### EARTH INCENSE (ELEMENTAL)

2 parts Pine resin (pitch) or needles
1 part Patchouly
1 pinch finely powdered Salt
a few drops Cypress oil

Burn for invoking the powers of the element of Earth for money, stability and so on. (See Part III for more information relating to the element of Earth.)

## EARTH INCENSE (PLANETARY)

1 part Pine needles
1 part Thyme
a few drops Patchouly oil

Burn to honor the Earth, and for all Earth-reverencing rituals (see Part III for details.)

## EGYPTIAN INCENSE

4 parts Frankincense
3 parts Gum Arabic
2 parts Myrrh
1 part Cedar
1 part Juniper
1 part Calamus
1 part Cinnamon

Burn during Egyptian rituals, or to honor any ancient Egyptian deity such as Isis, Osiris, Thoth, Anubis, Selket, Heket and so on.

## EIGHTFOLD HEARTH INCENSE

2 parts Dragon's Blood
2 parts Myrrh
1 part Juniper
1/2 part Sassafras
1/2 part Orange flowers
1/2 part Rose petals

Burn for a safe, warm, loving home. Also give as a gift to others.

### ESBAT INCENSE

4 parts Frankincense
3 parts Myrrh
2 parts Benzoin
1 part Sandalwood
1 part Gardenia petals
1/2 part Orris
1/2 part Thyme
1/2 part Poppy seed
1/2 part Rose petals

Burn during rituals and spells on the Full Moon, or at any Wiccan gathering other than the Sabbats (see Glossary).

### EXORCISM INCENSE

3 parts Frankincense
1 part Rosemary
1 part Bay
1 part Avens
1 part Mugwort
1 part St. John's Wort
1 part Angelica
1 part Basil

Burn with open windows in disturbed places as a heavy purificatory incense, and breathe through your mouth while smoldering this.

### FIRE INCENSE (ELEMENTAL)

3 parts Frankincense
2 parts Dragon's Blood
1 part Red Sandalwood
1 pinch Saffron
a few drops Musk oil

Smolder for summoning the powers and beings of Fire, and also for success, strength, protection, health, passion and other similar goals. Genuine saffron is prohibitively expensive; hence, the smallest pinch will suffice. If you have none in stock, substitute orange peel.

### FIRE OF AZRAEL

1 part Sandalwood
1 part Cedar
1 part Juniper

Burn while scrying, or throw onto the coals of a fire once the flames have been quenched and gaze into them to see images form within them. The latter rite is best performed on a beach at night. Fire of Azrael incense is also used as a general psychism-inducing incense.

### "FOR EMERGENCIES" INCENSE (*caution!*)
### (inspired by Jim Alan's song "Talkin' Wicca Blues"*)

3 parts Frankincense
2 parts Dragon's Blood
2 parts Myrrh
1 part Rosemary
1 part Asafoetida*
1 part Cayenne*
1 part Grains of Paradise
1 part Rue*
1 part Garlic*

Burn to be rid of foul demons, wrathful spirits, tax collectors, drunks, and other noisome creatures. Stand back and hold your nose—or better still, leave the room while this incense is smoldering. Those herbs marked with an asterisk above aren't necessarily dangerous or baneful, but they emit powerful smoke that is irritating to the eyes, nose and lungs.

### FULL MOON RITUAL INCENSE

3 parts Frankincense
1 part Sandalwood

Burn during Full Moon rituals, or simply to attune with the Moon.

---

* Write to Circle (you'll find their address in Appendix 2) for information on obtaining the tape *Circle Magick Music*, which includes this funny, clever song.

## FULL MOON RITUAL INCENSE # 2

2 parts Sandalwood
2 parts Frankincense
1/2 part Gardenia petals
1/4 part Rose petals
a few drops Ambergris oil

Another like the above.

## FULL MOON RITUAL INCENSE # 3

3 parts Gardenia petals
2 parts Frankincense
1 part Rose petals
1/2 part Orris
a few drops Sandalwood oil

A third like the above.

## GAMES OF CHANCE INCENSE

2 parts Gum Mastic
2 parts Frankincense

Burn before gambling.

## GEMINI INCENSE

2 parts Gum Mastic
1 part Citron (or 1 part mixed Orange and Lemon peel)
1/2 part Mace

Use as a personal altar or household incense to increase your powers.

## GREEK GOD AND GODDESS INCENSE

4 parts Frankincense (sacred to Apollo)
2 parts Myrrh (Demeter)
1 part Pine (Poseidon)
1 part Rose petals (Aphrodite)
1 part Sage (Zeus)
1 part White Willow bark (Persephone)

a few drops Olive oil (Athena)
a few drops Cypress oil (Artemis/Hecate)

Burn to honor Them.

## HEALING INCENSE

1 part Rosemary
1 part Juniper berries

Burn to speed healing while visualizing.

## HEALING INCENSE # 2

2 parts Myrrh
1 part Cinnamon
1 pinch Saffron

Another like the above.

## HEALING INCENSE # 3 (*caution!*)

3 parts Myrrh
2 parts Nutmeg
1 part Cedar
1 part Clove *
1/2 part Lemon Balm
1/2 part Poppy seeds
a few drops Pine oil
a few drops Almond oil

A third like the above.

## HEALING INCENSE # 4

3 parts Myrrh
1 part Rose Petals
1 part Eucalyptus
1 pinch Saffron
a few drops Cedarwood oil

## HEALING INCENSE # 5

2 parts Juniper berries
1 part Rosemary

## HECATE INCENSE

3 parts Sandalwood
2 parts Cypress
1 part Spearmint or Peppermint

To honor Her, burn at a crossroads or during ritual at the waning of the Moon.

## HONORS INCENSE

2 parts Benzoin
1 part Wood Aloe
1/2 part Pepperwort (or Rue)

Burn for honors and favors.

## HORNED GOD INCENSE

2 parts Benzoin
1 part Cedar
1 part Pine
1 part Juniper berries
a few drops Patchouly oil

Burn to honor Him in His many guises, especially during Wiccan rituals.

## HOUSE PURIFICATION INCENSE

3 parts Frankincense
2 parts Dragon's Blood
1 part Myrrh
1 part Sandalwood
1 part Wood Betony
1/2 part Dill seed
a few drops Rose Geranium oil

Burn in your home to cleanse it at least once a month, perhaps on the Full Moon. Additionally, burn this mixture in a new home before moving in.

## IMBOLC INCENSE

3 parts Frankincense
2 parts Dragon's Blood
1/2 part Red Sandalwood
1 part Cinnamon
a few drops Red Wine

To this mixture add a pinch of the first flower (dry it first) that is available in your area at the time of Imbolc (February 1st). Burn during Wiccan ceremonies on Imbolc, or simply to attune with the symbolic rebirth of the Sun—the fading of winter and the promise of spring.

## INCUBUS, INCENSE AGAINST THE (*caution!*)

2 parts Sandalwood
2 parts Benzoin
2 parts Wood Aloe
2 parts Cardamom
1/2 part Calamus
1/2 part Birthwort
1/2 part Ginger
1/2 part Pepper

1/2 part Cinnamon
1/2 part Clove*
1/2 part Carnation
1/2 part Nutmeg*
1/2 part Mace
1/2 part Cubeb seed
a few drops Brandy

This ancient mixture is burned to ward off the incubus (see Glossary).

## ISIS INCENSE

3 parts Myrrh
2 parts Sandalwood
1 part Frankincense
1 part Rose petals
a few drops Lotus bouquet (see Chapter 4)

Burn while reverencing Isis. Or, burn during any type of magical operation, since Isis is the Goddess of All Things.

## JUPITER INCENSE (PLANETARY)

2 parts Wood Aloe
1 part Benzoin
1 part Storax (or Gum Arabic)
1/4 part Ash seed
1 pinch powdered Lapis Lazuli
a few drops Olive oil

Mix and burn. This unusual formula includes a stone (lapis lazuli), and could also be mixed together and carried as a Jupiterian talisman charm. Burn for spells involving riches, expansion, the law and luck.

## JUPITER INCENSE # 2

3 parts Frankincense
1 part Mace
1 part Cardamom
1/2 part Balm of Gilead
1/4 part pulverized Oak leaves
1/8 part pulverized Pomegranate rind
1 pinch Saffron
a few drops Ambergris oil

Another like the above.

## JUPITER INCENSE # 3 (*caution!*)

1 part Clove*
1 part Nutmeg*
1 part Cinnamon
1/2 part Lemon Balm
1/2 part Citron peel (or equal parts dried Lemon and
    Orange peel)

A third like the above.

## KYPHI

| | |
|---|---|
| 4 parts Frankincense | 1/2 part Cinnamon |
| 2 parts Benzoin | 1/2 part Cassia |
| 2 parts Gum Mastic | 1/2 part Juniper berries |
| 2 parts Myrrh | 1/2 part Orris |
| 1 part Cedar | 1/2 part Cypress |
| 1 part Galangal (or Ginger) | a few drops Lotus bouquet |
| 1/2 part Calamus (or Vetivert) | a few drops Wine |
| 1/2 part Cardamom | a few drops Honey |
| | 7 raisins |

Mix the ground dry ingredients thoroughly. Let sit in an airtight container two weeks. In a separate bowl, mix together the oil, wine, honey and raisins. Add to the dry ingredients and blend with the hands. Let sit another two weeks. Then, if desired, grind to a fine powder. Kyphi is used in night rituals, to invoke Egyptian Goddesses and Gods, and as a general magical incense. (This recipe is a more refined version of the one that appeared in *Magical Herbalism*.)

## KYPHI # 2 (simplified)

| | |
|---|---|
| 3 parts Frankincense | 1/2 part Cedar |
| 2 parts Benzoin | 2 drops Lotus bouquet |
| 2 parts Myrrh | 2 drops Wine |
| 1 part Juniper berries | 2 drops Honey |
| 1/2 part Galangal | a few raisins |
| 1/2 part Cinnamon | |

Mix, burn, use as the above.

## LEO INCENSE

2 parts Gum Mastic
1 part Sandalwood
1 part Juniper berries

Use as a personal altar or household incense to increase your powers.

## LIBRA INCENSE

2 parts Sandalwood
1 part Thyme
a few drops Rose oil

Use as a personal altar or household incense to increase your powers.

## "LOCK" INCENSE

3 parts Frankincense
2 parts Juniper berries
1 part Vetivert
1/2 part Cumin

To guard your home from thieves: During the day smolder this mixture in a censer before the front door, then move it to each opening in the house (doors, windows, cellars, etc.) through which thieves may enter. Visualize its smoke forming an invisible but impenetrable barrier. Move in a clockwise circle throughout your home, replenishing the incense as necessary. Repeat monthly at the time of the Full Moon, if possible; or, use as needed. This incense is designed to "lock" your home against unwanted intruders—but don't forget to bolt your doors as well.

## LOVE INCENSE

2 parts Sandalwood
1/2 part Basil
1/2 part Bergamot
a few drops Rose oil
a few drops Lavender oil

Burn to attract love, to strengthen the love you have, and to expand your ability to give and to receive love.

## LOVE INCENSE # 2

2 parts Dragon's Blood
1 part Orris
1/2 part Cinnamon
1/2 part Rose petals
a few drops Musk oil
a few drops Patchouly oil

Another like the above.

## LUGHNASADH INCENSE

2 parts Frankincense
1 part Heather
1 part Apple blossoms
1 pinch Blackberry leaves
a few drops Ambergris oil

Burn Lughnasadh Incense during Wiccan rituals on August 1st or 2nd, or at that time to attune with the coming harvest.

## MABON INCENSE

2 parts Frankincense
1 part Sandalwood
1 part Cypress
1 part Juniper
1 part Pine
1/2 part Oakmoss (or a few drops Oakmoss bouquet)
1 pinch pulverized Oak leaf

Burn during Wiccan ceremonies on Mabon (the Autumnal Equinox, circa September 21st), or at that time to attune with the change of the seasons.

## MARS INCENSE (PLANETARY)

4 parts Benzoin
1 part Pine needles (or resin)
a scant pinch Black Pepper

Burn to attract its influences, or during spells involving lust, physical strength, competitions, rituals concerning men and so on.

## MARS INCENSE # 2 (*caution!*)

2 parts Galangal
1 part Coriander
1 part Clove*
1/2 part Basil
a scant pinch Black Pepper

Another like the above.

## MARS INCENSE # 3 (*caution!*)

2 parts Dragon's Blood
1 part Cardamom
1 part Clove*
1 part Grains of Paradise

A third like the above.

## MEDICINE WHEEL INCENSE

2 parts Sage
1 part Sweetgrass (see Appendix 2 for possible sources)
1 part Pine resin or needles
1 part Osha root (or Angelica root)
a scant pinch Tobacco

Burn during rites revering American Indian deities and spirits, and to attune with the energies of this land.

## MEDITATION INCENSE

1 part Gum Acacia (or Gum Arabic)
1 part Sandalwood

Burn a small amount prior to meditation to relax the conscious mind.

## MERCURY INCENSE (PLANETARY)

2 parts Benzoin
1 part Mace
1/2 part Marjoram
a few drops Lavender oil

Burn to invoke its powers, or during spells involving intelligence, travel, divination and so on. (See Part III for more information regarding the magical powers of Mercury.)

## MERCURY INCENSE # 2

2 parts Benzoin
1 part Frankincense
1 part Mace

Another like the above.

## MERCURY INCENSE # 3

2 parts Sandalwood
1 part Gum Mastic
1/2 part Lavender (or a few drops Lavender oil)

A third like the above.

## MEXICAN MAGIC INCENSE

2 parts Copal
1 part Frankincense
1 part Rosemary

Smolder during Mexican-American folk magic rituals and spells.

## MIDSUMMER INCENSE

2 parts Sandalwood
1 part Mugwort
1 part Camomile
1 part Gardenia petals
a few drops Rose oil
a few drops Lavender oil
a few drops Yarrow oil

Burn at Wiccan rituals at the Summer Solstice (circa June 21st) or at that time to attune with the seasons and the Sun.

## MIDSUMMER INCENSE # 2

3 parts Frankincense
2 parts Benzoin
1 part Dragon's Blood
1 part Thyme
1 part Rosemary
1 pinch Vervain
a few drops Red Wine

Another like the above.

## MOON INCENSE

2 parts Frankincense
1 part Sandalwood
a few drops Eucalyptus oil
a few drops Jasmine oil
a few drops Camphor oil

Burn to attract its influences, and also during psychic workings, love magic, healing, rituals involving the home and dream magic.

### MOON INCENSE # 2

4 parts Sandalwood
2 parts Wood Aloe
1 part Eucalyptus
1 part pulverized Cucumber seed
1 part Mugwort
1/2 part Ranunculus blossoms
1 part Selenetrope
a few drops Ambergris oil

I still don't know what selenetrope is; substitute gardenia or jasmine.

### MOON INCENSE # 3

2 parts Juniper berries
1 part Orris
1 part Calamus
a few drops Spirits of Camphor (or Camphor tincture; or
    1/4 part genuine Camphor)
a few drops Lotus bouquet

A third like the above.

### MOON INCENSE # 4

2 parts Myrrh
2 parts Gardenia petals
1 part Rose petals
1 part Lemon peel
1/2 part Camphor
a few drops Jasmine oil

### MOONFIRE INCENSE

1 part Rose
1 part Orris
1 part Bay
1 part Juniper
1 part Dragon's Blood
1/2 part Potassium Nitrate

Burn for divination, love and harmony. The potassium nitrate is included in this incense to make it sparkle and glow. If you add too much it will explode!

### NINE WOODS INCENSE

1 part Rowan wood (or Sandalwood)
1 part Apple wood
1 part Dogwood
1 part Poplar wood
1 part Juniper wood
1 part Cedar wood
1 part Pine wood
1 part Holly branches
1 part Elder (or Oak) wood

Take sawdust of each, mix together, and burn indoors on charcoal when a ritual fire is necessary or desired but not practical. The incense emits the aroma of an open campfire.

### OFFERTORY INCENSE

2 parts Frankincense
1 part Myrrh
1 part Cinnamon
1/2 part Rose petals
1/2 part Vervain

Burn while honoring the Goddesses and Gods, and as an offering.

## OSTARA INCENSE

2 parts Frankincense
1 part Benzoin
1 part Dragon's Blood
1/2 part Nutmeg
1/2 part Violet flowers (or a few drops Violet oil)
1/2 part Orange peel
1/2 part Rose petals

Burn during Wiccan rituals on Ostara (the Spring Equinox, which varies from March 20th to the 24th each year), or to welcome the spring and to refresh your life.

## PELE INCENSE

2 parts Frankincense
1 part Dragon's Blood
1 part Red Sandalwood
1 part Orange peel
1 part Cinnamon
a few drops Clove oil

Burn while honoring Pele,* the Hawaiian goddess of volcanoes; when needing additional strength for any ritual; when you feel manipulated by others, or for Fire spells in general. Burn when you wish to be filled with the power of Pele.

## PISCES INCENSE

2 parts Frankincense
1 part Eucalyptus
1 part Lemon peel
a few drops Sandalwood oil

Use as a personal altar or household incense to increase your powers.

---

\* Pele isn't just a goddess of destruction. She's also a goddess of creation, a true Mother Goddess, since she creates new land every time one of Her lava flows reaches the sea. She is a powerful deity still respected in present-day Hawaii.

### A GENERAL PLANETARY INCENSE (*caution!*)

| | |
|---|---|
| 1 part Myrrh | 1 part Frankincense |
| 1 part Gum Mastic | 1 part Camphor |
| 1 part Costus | 1 part Red Sandalwood |
| 1 part Opoponax | 1 part Wood Aloe |
| 1 part Storax | 1 part Euphorbium* |
| 1 part Thyme | |

For general magical workings. The baneful substance in this recipe, euphorbium, can be replaced with tobacco. Gum arabic can be used in place of the storax, as mentioned previously. Gum opoponax is virtually unobtainable; use an opoponax oil or substitute with gum arabic.

### PROPHECY INCENSE (*caution!*)

1 part Fleawort seed
1 part Violet root
1 part Parsley
1 part Hempseed*

Burn for divination and psychic work.

### PROPHETIC DREAM INCENSE

2 parts Frankincense
1 part Buchu

Burn before bedtime to stimulate the psychic mind to produce future-revealing dreams, and to ensure that the conscious mind remembers them in the morning.

### PROSPERITY INCENSE

2 parts Frankincense
1 part Cinnamon
1 part Nutmeg
1 part Lemon Balm
1 part Citron

Burn to attract wealth.

## PROTECTION INCENSE

2 parts Frankincense
1 part Dragon's Blood
1/2 part Wood Betony

Burn for both physical and psychic protection while visualizing.

## PROTECTION INCENSE # 2

2 parts Frankincense
1 part Sandalwood
1/2 part Rosemary

Another like the above.

## PROTECTION INCENSE # 3 (*caution!*)

1 part Frankincense
1 part Myrrh
1/2 part Clove*

A third like the above.

## PROTECTION INCENSE # 4

2 parts Frankincense
1/2 part Cumin

## PROTECTION INCENSE # 5

4 parts Frankincense     1/2 part Mugwort
3 parts Myrrh            1/2 part Yarrow
2 parts Juniper berries  1/2 part St. John's Wort
1 part Rosemary          1/2 part Angelica
1/2 part Avens           1/2 part Basil

## PROTECTION INCENSE #6

2 parts Frankincense
1 part Copal
1 part Dragon's Blood

## PSYCHIC INCENSE

3 parts Frankincense
1 part Bistort

Smolder to sharpen psychic powers.

## PSYCHIC INCENSE # 2

2 parts Sandalwood
1 part Gum Acacia (or Gum Arabic)

Another like the above.

## PSYCHIC INCENSE # 3 (*caution!*)

1 part Frankincense
1 part Sandalwood
1 part Cinnamon
1 part Nutmeg*
a few drops Orange oil
a few drops Clove oil

## PURIFICATION INCENSE (*caution!*)

4 parts Frankincense
2 parts Bay
1 part Camphor
1 pinch finely powdered Salt
1 pinch Sulfur*

Burn to purify the atmosphere of a disturbed home. Leave the windows open and do not inhale the sulphurous fumes!

## PURIFICATION INCENSE # 2

2 parts Sandalwood
1 part Cinnamon

Another like the above. Though no sulfur is included in this formula, it's best to leave the windows open during all types of purification rites.

## PURIFICATION INCENSE # 3

3 parts Frankincense
1 part Vervain

A third like the above.

## RAIN INCENSE (*caution!*)

4 parts Heather
1 part Fern
1/2 part Henbane*

Burn out of doors on a deserted hill to attract rain. Do not inhale fumes!

## "RAISE THE DEAD" INCENSE

1 part Pepperwort
1 part Red Storax
1 pinch Saffron
a few drops Musk oil

Compound and fumigate about the tombs and graves of the dead. This will cause spirits and ghosts to gather, at least according to ancient writings.

## RICHES AND FAVORS INCENSE (*caution!*)

2 parts Benzoin
1 part Wood Aloe
1/2 part Pepperwort
1/2 part Clove *

Burn when you need favors and wealth.

## SABBAT INCENSE (*caution!*)

4 parts Frankincense

2 parts Myrrh

2 parts Benzoin

1/2 part Bay

1/2 part Fennel

1/2 part Thyme

1/2 part Pennyroyal

1/2 part Solomon's Seal

1/4 part Rue*

1/4 part Wormwood *

1/4 part Camomile

1/4 part Rose petals

Burn at Wiccan Sabbats.

## SAGITTARIUS INCENSE (*caution!*)

2 parts Frankincense

1 part Myrrh

1 part Clove*

Use as a personal altar or household incense to increase your own powers.

## SAHUMERIA AZTECA INCENSE

3 parts Copal

2 parts Frankincense

1 part Rosemary

1 part Sage

1 part Lemongrass

1 part Bay

1/2 part Marigold

1/2 part Yerba Santa

For ancient Aztecan rituals and all Mexican-American folk magic. Also, use as a general purification incense. I first learned of this mixture a decade ago from a Latina who owned an herb shop not far from my home. Later I found it for sale in *botanicas* (herb and occult supply shops) in Tijuana. It's a famous incense in contemporary Mexican folk magic.

### SATURN INCENSE (PLANETARY) (*caution!*)

2 parts Frankincense
2 parts Poppy seed
1 part Gum Arabic
1 part Myrrh
1/4 part Henbane seed*
1/4 part Mandrake*
a few drops Olive Oil

Burn for Saturnian influences; also for spells dealing with buildings, studying past lives, banishing illnesses, pests and negative habits. This incense can be hazardous to your health; for a recommended Saturnian incense see formula #3 below *or* substitute 1/2 part tobacco for the henbane and mandrake listed above.

### SATURN INCENSE # 2 (*caution!*)

2 parts Cypress
2 parts Ash leaves
1 part Alum
1 part Gum Scammony
1 part Asafoetida*
1 part Sulphur*
1/4 part Black Nightshade*

Another like the above, but not recommended. By omitting the black nightshade, the incense is fairly innocuous but still smells incredibly foul!

### SATURN INCENSE # 3

2 parts Sandalwood
2 parts Myrrh
1 part Dittany of Crete
a few drops Cypress oil
a few drops Patchouly oil

This is the recommended Saturn incense formula. If you're going to use one of these four, this should be it!

### SATURN INCENSE # 4 (caution!)

1 part Pepperwort
1 part Mandrake*
1 part Myrrh
a few drops Musk oil

### SCORPIO INCENSE

2 parts Frankincense
1 part Galangal
1 part Pine resin (pitch)

Use as a personal altar or household incense to increase your powers.

### SCRYING INCENSE (caution!)

1 part Mugwort
1 part Wormwood*

Burn a small amount prior to scrying in a quartz crystal sphere, in flames, water and so on. Be warned—this one doesn't smell so good.

### SIGHT INCENSE

2 parts Gum Mastic
2 parts Juniper
1 part Sandalwood
1 part Cinnamon
1 part Calamus
a few drops Ambergris oil
a few drops Patchouly oil

Mix, empower and burn to promote psychic awareness. This is another version of the recipe that appeared in *Magical Herbalism*. Other variants include hemp.

## SPIRIT INCENSE (*caution!*)

4 parts Coriander
1 part Smallage (Parsley)
1/4 part Henbane*
1/4 part Hemlock*

Burn outdoors to draw spirits together. As usual, do not inhale fumes!

## SPIRIT INCENSE # 2 (*caution!*)

root of the weedy herb Sagapen (?)
juice of Hemlock*
juice of Henbane*
*Tapsus barbatus* (?)
Red Sandalwood
Black Poppy seed

Fume to make spirits and strange shapes appear. To make them flee, add parsley to this mixture, as this chases away all spirits and destroys all visions (which seems to contradict Spirit Incense #1 above!) This 500-year-old formula is virtually impossible to compound. I included this recipe as an example of an authentic, ancient herbal incense. Most of these are as difficult to make as this one. What is the "weedy herb Sagapen"? I haven't the slightest idea!

## SPIRIT INCENSE # 3

1 part Anise
1 part Coriander
1 part Cardamom

Smolder to cause spirits to gather.

## SPIRIT INCENSE #4

1 part Sandalwood
1 part Lavender

Burn on the altar to invite good energies (or spirits) to be present during magical rituals.

### SPIRIT INCENSE #5

2 parts Sandalwood
1 part Willow bark

Burn out of doors at night during the Waxing Moon.

### SPIRIT INCENSE # 6

3 parts Wood Aloe
1 part Costus
1 part Crocus
a few drops Ambergris oil
a few drops Musk oil

### SPIRIT INCENSE #7 (*caution!*)

3 parts Frankincense
2 parts Coriander
1 part Fennel root
1 part Cassia
1/2 part Henbane*

Take all ingredients to a dark, haunted, enchanted forest. Sprinkle dried mullein or patchouly on an old tree stump. On this set black candles, a censer and the incense. Light the tapers, burn the incense and wait until the candles are suddenly extinguished. There in the darkness around you will be the spirits. To be rid of them, burn asafoetida or frankincense.

So you're wondering why I included seven spirit incenses in this book? Well, they're traditional. I'm not recommending anyone to actually use these recipes; again, they're a part of the colorful heritage of the magical herbalist and of magicians in general. To reiterate Chapter 1, magic isn't performed through the use of spirits. Magic is a direction of personal power (the energy within), as well as of Earth power (that resident in plants and stones) to effect needed goals. Besides, what would you do with all those spirits if they did indeed appear?

## SPIRITS DEPART INCENSE (*caution!*)

1 part Calamint
1 part Peony
1 part Mint (Spearmint)
1/4 part Castor Beans*

Burn out of doors to drive away all evil spirits and vain imaginings. If you wish to use this formula, substitute a few drops castor oil for the beans, as these are poisonous.

## SPIRITS DEPART INCENSE #2

2 parts Fennel seed
2 parts Dill seed
1/2 part Rue

Another like the above.

## STUDY INCENSE

2 parts Gum Mastic
1 part Rosemary

Smolder to strengthen the conscious mind for study, to develop concentration and to improve the memory.

## SUCCESS INCENSE (*caution!*)

3 parts Wood Aloe
2 parts Red Storax
1 part Nutmeg*

Burn for success in all undertakings. Since red storax (indeed, all storax) is unavailable, substitute frankincense or gum arabic.

## SUN INCENSE

3 parts Frankincense        1/2 part Carnation
2 parts Myrrh               a few drops Ambergris oil
1 part Wood Aloe            a few drops Musk oil
1/2 part Balm of Gilead     a few drops Olive oil
1/2 part Bay

Burn to draw the influences of the Sun and for spells involving promotions, friendship, healing, energy and magical power.

## SUN INCENSE #2

3 parts Frankincense
2 parts Sandalwood
1 part Bay
1 pinch Saffron
a few drops Orange oil

Another like the above.

## SUN INCENSE #3 (*caution!*)

3 parts Frankincense
2 parts Galangal
2 parts Bay
1/4 part Mistletoe*
a few drops Red Wine
a few drops Honey

A third like the above.

### TALISMAN CONSECRATION INCENSE (*caution!*)

Alum
Gum Scammony
Asafoetida*
Sulphur*
Cypress
Black Hellebore*
Ash leaves

Burn in an earthen dish and hold the talismans in the smoke. I've refrained from including proportions in this recipe because I don't recommend its use. Try the following nonpoisonous version or the Consecration Incense to consecrate all forms of amulets and talismans.

### TALISMAN CONSECRATION INCENSE (nontoxic version)

2 parts Frankincense
1 part Cypress
1 part Ash leaves
1 part Tobacco
1 pinch Valerian
1 pinch Alum
1 pinch Asafoetida*

Though this one won't kill you, like the above version it still stinks. I heartily recommend the Consecration Incense.

### TAURUS INCENSE

2 parts Sandalwood
2 parts Benzoin
a few drops Rose oil

Use as a personal altar or household incense to increase your powers.

## TEMPLE INCENSE

3 parts Frankincense
2 parts Myrrh
a few drops Lavender oil
a few drops Sandalwood oil

Smolder in the temple or "magic room," or as a general magical incense. This incense increases spirituality.

## THIEF INCENSE (to see a thief)

1 part Crocus
1 pinch Alum

In ancient Egypt this mixture was placed on a brazier and the seer stared into the coals.

## THOUSAND-NAMED SOLAR INCENSE (*caution!*)

3 parts Frankincense
1 part Clove*
1/2 part Red Sandalwood
1/2 part Sandalwood
1/4 part Orange flowers
3 pinches Orris

Burn for Solar influences (see Part III).

## TRUE LOVE INCENSE

1 part Cinnamon
1 part Orris
a few drops Patchouly oil

Burn for love.

## UNIVERSAL INCENSE

3 parts Frankincense
2 parts Benzoin
1 part Myrrh
1 part Sandalwood
1 part Rosemary

Burn for all positive magical purposes. If this formula is used for negative magical goals, the incense will cancel out the spell or ritual.

## VENUS INCENSE (PLANETARY)

3 parts Wood Aloe
1 part Red Rose petals
1 pinch crushed Red Coral (optional)
a few drops Olive oil
a few drops Musk oil
a few drops Ambergris oil

Mix well and burn for Venusian influences, such as love, healing, partnerships and rituals involving women. The inclusion of coral in this recipe dates it to about the 16th century, when coral was considered to be a powerful love stimulant. Now that we know that coral is the skeleton of a living creature, it's best to omit it entirely.

## VENUS INCENSE #2

1 part Violets
1 part Rose petals
1/2 part Olive leaves

Another like the above.

### VENUS INCENSE #3

2 parts Sandalwood
2 parts Benzoin
1 part Rosebuds
a few drops Patchouly oil
a few drops Rose oil

A third like the above.

### VIRGO INCENSE

1 part Mace
1 part Cypress
a few drops Patchouly oil

Use as a personal altar or household incense to increase your powers.

### VISION INCENSE

3 parts Frankincense
1 part Bay
1/2 part Damiana

Burn a small amount prior to psychic workings.

### VISION INCENSE #2 (*caution!*)

1 part Calamus
1 part Fennel root
1 part Pomegranate skin
1 part Red Sandalwood
1 part Black Poppy seeds
1/2 part Henbane*

Another like the above, but not recommended.

### WATER INCENSE (ELEMENTAL)

2 parts Benzoin
1 part Myrrh
1 part Sandalwood
a few drops Lotus bouquet
a few drops Ambergris oil

Burn to attract the influences of this element, as well as to develop psychism, to promote love, fertility, beauty and so on.

### WEALTH INCENSE

1 part Nutmeg
1 part Pepperwort
1 pinch Saffron

Burn to attract wealth.

### WEALTH INCENSE #2

2 parts Pine needles or resin
1 part Cinnamon
1 part Galangal
a few drops Patchouly oil

Another like the above.

### WEALTH INCENSE #3 (*caution!*)

2 parts Frankincense
1 part Cinnamon
1 part Nutmeg
1/2 part Clove*
1/2 part Ginger
1/2 part Mace

A third like the above.

## YULE INCENSE

2 parts Frankincense
2 parts Pine needles or resin
1 part Cedar
1 part Juniper berries

Mix and smolder at Wiccan rites on Yule (on or around December 21st), or during the winter months to cleanse the home and to attune with the forces of nature amid the cold days and nights.

# *Oils*

IT HAS BECOME quite popular to use essential oils for magical purposes. Blends such as Controlling Oil and Come to Me Essence are in daily use by many practitioners of Voodoo-flavored folk magic.

Such practices, often thought of as being ancient, do indeed date back thousands of years in one form or another; but not until recently were the array of true and synthetic botanical oils available for ritual purposes.

Scented oils were used in antiquity. These were created by heating fragrant plant materials in oil or fat. The plant's scent was transferred to the oil and thus was fragranced.

Many people tell me that they want to make their own oils. Unfortunately, this is a difficult process. Why? Here are a few reasons:

*It requires a large investment in equipment.* Much of this must be specially adapted for this purpose. Condensers, fractionating columns and other exotica are necessary and expensive.

*It requires a large amount of fresh plant materials.* Do you have a couple hundred pounds of, say, fresh tuberose petals? Additionally, the petals, leaves or roots must be of the appropriate species. For example, the best rose oils are created from the "old world" varieties, which are rarely available in large quantities.

*The process must be carefully carried out to exacting standards.* If just one step is missed or overlooked—if, perhaps, the temperature reaches an inappropriate high or low—the oil will be of lesser quality.

*Often the results aren't worth the investment of time and money.* Homemade carnation oil certainly won't smell like carnations.

There are few plant oils that can be extracted at home without much difficulty. For the rest, simply buy and blend high quality oils for ritual use.

## Buying Oils

Numerous companies offer oils for purchase. Some of these sell only genuine, authentic *essential* oils—i.e., those extracted from the natural botanical material after which they're named (lavender oil made from lavender, for example). Many others sell *blends*, compounds or bouquets, which reproduce a specific scent by mixing various true essential oils (see Chapter 4 for examples of bouquets). Most companies offer either partially or totally *synthetic* oils, though they're never labelled as such.

It's best to use only genuine, authentic essential oils in magic. These contain the sum of the plant's magical energies and so are the most effective. True, they aren't cheap, but they last longer because only small amounts are necessary. It is expensive to build up a good stock of genuine essential oils, but this is necessary to create quality magical oils.

I have worked with synthetics for years. Some of them are effective but pale in comparison with the aromas and power of true essential oils. Remember not to be fooled by the "essential oil" tags which manufacturers often attach to synthetic scents. Buying from the mail-order sources that sell essential oils listed in Appendix 2, or from retail stores that stock these oils, is virtually your only assurance of getting the real thing.

I know that some of you will continue to use synthetic oils. However, if my words here convince a few of you to make the great leap into the world of truly *natural* magic I'll be happy.

For those fragrances unavailable in essential oil form (such as tuberose, sweet pea and others) see Chapter 4 for recipes of bouquets that can be blended from true essential oils and used in place of, say, lotus.

## Blending Oils

There's no magic secret for blending and mixing magical oils. Here's the basic method:

• Assemble the essential oils (and bouquets) called for in the recipe.

• In a clean, sterilized glass jar, add 1/8 cup of one of the following vegetable oils:

| | |
|---|---|
| Safflower | Almond |
| Sunflower | Hazelnut |
| Coconut | Grapeseed |
| Apricot Kernel | |
| Jojoba | |

I've found jojoba is the best to use. Because it isn't truly an oil but a liquid form of wax, it never becomes rancid and can be kept for longer periods of time.

• Using an eye dropper or the convenient single-drop dispensers which are included in virtually every bottle of true essential oil, add the essential oils in the proportions recommended in the recipes that follow.

• Swirl the essential oils into the base oil, don't stir. Gently rotate the oil clockwise.

• Finally, store all oils away from heat, light and moisture (not in the bathroom) in airtight, opaque or dark-colored glass bottles. Label and keep for use.

*AN EXAMPLE*

We'll make Fast Money Oil. Here's the recipe:

FAST MONEY OIL

7 drops Patchouly
5 drops Cedarwood
4 drops Vetivert
2 drops Ginger

While visualizing my magical goal—money—I add 1/8 cup jojoba oil to a sterilized glass jar. In front of me on the table I've placed jars of patchouly, cedarwood, vetivert and ginger essential oils—not synthetics.

I visualize money. I add seven drops patchouly to the jojoba and swirl to mix it in with the base oil. I sniff. The fragrance has overpowered the light odor of the pure jojoba oil.

Visualize. Add five drops cedarwood. Swirl. Sniff. The scent is building.

Four drops of vetivert essential oil follow. While visualizing, swirl. Sniff. The aroma of the magical oil in the making deepens as the three fragrances and their energies mingle.

Finally, the ginger essential oil. This is such a strong, heady scent that only two drops are required. I mix again, smell again, visualize again. After a short empowering rite the magical Fast Money Oil is ready for use.

It is a rich, evocative scent. Used with visualization it will be effective in manifesting an increased cash flow.

Could I make this with synthetics? Of course. Would it be as effective? No.

### Using Oils

Oils are used in innumerable ways in magic. Remember: Always use oils with visualization and with power.

Most often, they're rubbed onto candles which are then burned in ritual. The magical goal determines the type of oil and the color of the candle used. The oil's powers mix with that of the color and the candle flame. All these energies are further boosted by the magician's personal power and are sped toward the magical goal through visualization.

Oils are also simply used to anoint the body to bring their energies within. Thus, rubbing a Love Oil onto the wrists, the neck, and over the heart infuses the magician with love-attracting energies. Courage Oil similarly imbues her or him with the strength to forge ahead in the face of adversity.

A simple bath can be transformed into a ritual by adding several drops of oil to the water. Slipping into it and inhaling the fragrance, the magician once again brings the oil's energies inside.

Talismans and amulets (often termed "charms" or "sachets") may be anointed with a few drops of the appropriate mixed oil. This is done, of course, with the specific magical goal in mind.

Quartz crystals and other stones are also rubbed with oils to boost their energies during spells and rituals. The stones are then worn, carried or placed in mystic patterns to bring about specific magical goals.

Other ritual uses of oils will become apparent once you start using them.

## *A Guide to True Essential Oils and Bouquets*

This is an alphabetical listing of the magical properties of the most commonly used essential oils and bouquets. No synthetics have been included here. They can be used by themselves for any of the purposes mentioned directly above, but true essential oils should be diluted before applying them to the skin.

### *Diluting True Essential Oils*

As a general guideline, add 5 to 7 drops to 1/8 cup of base oil, such as jojoba. This dilutes the essential oil so that it won't irritate the skin, but you will still be able to smell it.

Some true essential oils are such severe skin irritants that I've rarely included them in any of the recipes in this section, and have noted this property below.

For more in-depth magical information concerning true essential oils, see *Magical Aromatherapy: The Power of Scent* (Cunningham, Llewellyn Publications, 1989).

APRICOT OIL: This oil, pressed from apricot kernels, is aphrodisiac in nature. It is used as a base for mixing true essential oils but does not have an apricot-like scent.

BASIL: The scent of basil causes sympathy between two persons and so is worn to avoid major clashes. Basil essential oil is useful in blends for encouraging happiness and peace and for stimulating the conscious mind. It is fine in money-attracting magical oils, which might be why prostitutes once wore it in Spain to attract customers.

BENZOIN: This is a rich, thick essential oil with a natural vanilla-like scent. Dilute and rub onto the body to increase your personal power. It awakens the conscious mind as well.

BERGAMOT MINT BOUQUET: Use for money and protective rituals. Add the diluted bouquet to your bath water for these purposes.

BLACK PEPPER: Use the essential oil for protection and to promote courage. It has a sharp, sweet scent and is best added to blends rather than worn alone, even if diluted.

CAMOMILE: A fruity, incredibly full scent. Sparingly use camomile essential oil for meditation and inducing peace. Expensive but worth it!

CAMPHOR: The cooly scented essential oil is fine for purification and promoting celibacy.

CARDAMOM: Deliciously spicy, cardamom essential oil brings a nice jolt of energy to love and sexually oriented formulas.

CEDARWOOD: This essential oil has a woodsy scent. Its energies are useful in enhancing spirituality.

CINNAMON: True cinnamon oil is irritating to the skin. Use sparingly in money and psychic awareness blends—no more than one drop!

CLOVE OIL: Another irritant. Add one drop to 1/8 cup of base oil. Useful in courage and protection blends.

CORIANDER: Coriander essential oil works well in love and healing mixtures.

CYPRESS: Cypress is an essential oil of blessing, consecration and protection. This unique scent stimulates healing and eases the pain of losses of all kinds.

EUCALYPTUS: Perhaps the ultimate healing oil. Add to all healing blends. Apply (undiluted, in this case) to the body to relieve colds. Also used in purification mixtures.

FRANKINCENSE: An incredibly rich scent, frankincense essential oil is useful in promoting spirituality and meditative states. Dilute before applying to the skin; it may be irritating.

GERANIUM, ROSE: This essential oil (usually sold simply as "Geranium") is a powerful protectant. Wear diluted, or add to happiness blends.

GINGER: Powerfully spicy. Ginger essential oil is useful in sexuality, love, courage and money-attracting blends.

GRAPEFRUIT: The essential oil is a powerful purifier and is added to purification fragrances.

JASMINE: Symbolic of the Moon and of the mysteries of the night. Jasmine essential oil (or absolute) is a wonderfully evocative aroma. Though incredibly expensive, one precious drop can be added to love, psychic awareness, peace and spirituality blends. It is also useful for sexuality. Do, however, avoid synthetic jasmines!

JUNIPER: The resinous essential oil is useful in protection, purification and healing blends.

LAVENDER: This clean, refreshing essential oil is included in health, love, peace and conscious mind-oriented formulas.

LEMON: Use in Lunar oils. Wear diluted lemon oil during the Full Moon to attune with its energies. Use in purification and healing oils.

LEMONGRASS: This essential oil strengthens psychic awareness and is also useful in purification mixtures.

LEMON VERBENA: Often sold simply as "Verbena," this full, lemon-scented essential oil is wonderful in love blends.

LIME: A refreshing scent, useful in purification and protection.

LOTUS BOUQUET: Add the diluted bouquet to formulas designed to promote spirituality, healing or meditation.

MAGNOLIA BOUQUET: An excellent addition to meditation and psychic awareness oils, as well as love mixtures.

MYRRH: The essential oil can be added to blends designed to enhance spirituality and meditation. It is also often used in healing mixtures.

NEROLI: Also known as Orange Flower essential oil. A fabulously rich, citrous scent, neroli essential oil is quite expensive. However, a drop added to happiness and purification blends works wonders.

NEW-MOWN HAY BOUQUET: Add a few drops of the bouquet to transformative oils, especially those designed to break negative habits and addictions. Also, anoint the body in the spring with this bouquet (diluted, of course) to welcome the turning of the seasons.

NIAOULI: The remarkably exotic scent of niaouli essential oil is excellent when used in protection formulas.

OAKMOSS BOUQUET: Use to attract money. Dilute and wear or rub onto cash before spending.

ORANGE: A highly Solar scent, orange essential oil is added to purification blends.

PALMAROSA: A unique essential oil, palmarosa smells like a combination of citrus and rose. Useful for love and healing.

PATCHOULY: Useful in money, sex and physical energy blends. Or, dilute and wear for these purposes.

PEPPERMINT: This familiar scent is excellent when used for purification.

PETITGRAIN: A protective, bitter orange scent. This essential oil is useful in protective blends.

PINE: The resinous scent of pine is commonly added to purification, protection, money and healing formulas.

ROSE: The accepted love scent. True rose essential oil (known as *otto*) and rose absolute (a different form) are expensive but, as with jasmine, one drop has powerful scenting properties. Rose essential oil is used in formulas designed to attract love, confer peace, stimulate sexual desires and enhance beauty. Do not use synthetics!

ROSEMARY: The familiar aroma of the culinary herb is captured in its essential oil form. Add to love and healing magical blends.

SANDALWOOD: This ancient, sacred scent is used in spirituality, meditation, sex and healing formulas. Or, dilute and wear to bring these influences inside you.

SWEET PEA BOUQUET: Diluted with a base oil, sweet pea bouquet is worn to attract new friends and to draw love, and so it is also used in such blends.

TANGERINE: An energy scent drenched with the powers of the Sun. Add tangerine essential oil to power and strength mixtures.

TONKA BOUQUET: This warm, vanilla-like scent can be included in money recipes.

TUBEROSE BOUQUET: This bouquet is a wonderful relaxer, and so is used in peace blends. The scent also induces love.

VETIVERT: A money scent. Add to such mixtures or dilute and wear. Anoint cash before spending.

YARROW: One of the true treasures of the Earth, yarrow essential oil is naturally blue, possesses an incredible scent, and can be added in small amounts (due to its price) to love, courage and psychic-awareness blends.

YLANG-YLANG: The rich, tropical aroma of this essential oil is useful in promoting love, peace and sex. It can be worn on the body or included in such mixtures.

## *The Recipes*

Once again, the proportions listed here are the *suggested* ones. If you wish to deviate from these, simply keep in mind that the first ingredient listed should generally constitute the main scent. Each succeeding ingredient should be added in consecutively smaller amounts.

Remember:
- add these essential oils to 1/8 cup of a base oil
- visualize as you mix and smell
- for best results, don't use synthetics

### AIR OIL (ELEMENTAL)

5 drops Lavender
3 drops Sandalwood
1 drop Neroli

Wear to invoke the powers of Air and to promote clear thinking, for travel spells, and to overcome addictions. (See Part III for more information regarding the elements.)

## ALTAR OIL

4 drops Frankincense
2 drops Myrrh
1 drop Cedar

Anoint the altar with this oil at regular intervals, calling your Deity (Deities) to watch over it.

## ANOINTING OIL

5 drops Sandalwood
3 drops Cedarwood
1 drop Orange
1 drop Lemon

Use for general ritual anointing purposes.

## ANOINTING OIL #2

5 drops Myrrh
2 drops Cinnamon

Another like the last.

## APHRODITE OIL

5 drops Cypress
2 drops Cinnamon
a small piece of dried Orris root

Add the true essential oils and the orris root to an *olive-oil* base. Anoint your body to bring a love into your life.

## AQUARIUS OIL

5 drops Lavender
1 drop Cypress
1 drop Patchouly

Wear as a personal oil to increase your own powers.

### ARIES OIL

3 drops Frankincense
1 drop Ginger
1 drop Black Pepper
1 drop Petitgrain

Wear as a personal oil to increase your own powers.

### ASTRAL TRAVEL OIL

5 drops Sandalwood
1 drop Ylang-Ylang
1 drop Cinnamon

Add these to the base oil as usual and mix. Anoint the stomach, wrists, back of the neck and forehead (but remember—these essential oils are added to a base). Lie down and visualize yourself astrally projecting.*

### BUSINESS SUCCESS OIL

3 parts Bergamot Mint Bouquet
1 part Basil
1 part Patchouly
1 pinch of ground Cinnamon

Mix the oils and add the pinch of ground cinnamon to the base oil. Anoint the hands, cash register, business card or the front door of the place of business to increase cash flow.

### CANCER OIL (MOONCHILDREN)

4 drops Palmarosa
1 drop Camomile
1 drop Yarrow

Wear as a personal oil to increase your own powers.

---

* Denning and Phillip's *Astral Projection* (Llewellyn Publications, 1979) is an excellent guide.

### CAPRICORN OIL

3 drops Vetivert
2 drops Cypress
1 drop Patchouly

Wear as a personal oil to increase your own powers.

### CITRUS PURIFICATION OIL

3 drops Orange
2 drops Lemongrass
2 drops Lemon
1 drop Lime

Anoint white candles and burn in the home to purify it.

### COME AND SEE ME OIL

5 drops Patchouly
1 drop Cinnamon

To attract the ideal mate, mix these true essential oils in an olive-oil base, smear on a white image candle of the appropriate sex, and burn with visualization.

### COURAGE OIL

3 drops Ginger
1 drop Black Pepper
1 drop Clove

Wear to increase your courage, especially before being introduced to people, prior to public speaking, and other nerve-wracking situations.

### DEMETER OIL

3 drops Myrrh
2 drops Vetivert
1 drop Oakmoss Bouquet

Anoint to attract money and for the successful completion of your protections and dreams. Also wear when planting, tending, harvesting or working with herbs and plants to ensure a fruitful yield. Helps us tune in with the energies of the Earth.

### EARTH OIL (ELEMENTAL)

4 drops Patchouly
4 drops Cypress

Wear to invoke the powers of the Earth to bring money, prosperity, abundance, stability and foundation. (See Part III for more elemental information.)

### ENERGY OIL

4 drops Orange
2 drops Lime
1 drop Cardamom

Wear when feeling depleted, when ill, or just to strengthen your own energy reserves. Especially useful after heavy magical ritual to recharge your bodily batteries.

### FAST MONEY OIL

7 drops Patchouly
5 drops Cedarwood
4 drops Vetivert
2 drops Ginger

Wear, rub on the hands, or anoint green candles to bring money. Also anoint money before spending to ensure its return.

### FAST MONEY OIL # 2

4 drops Basil
2 drops Ginger
1 drop Tonka Bouquet

Another like the last.

## FIRE OIL (ELEMENTAL)

3 drops Ginger
2 drops Rosemary
1 drop Clove
1 drop Petitgrain

Wear to invoke the powers of Fire, such as energy, courage, strength, love, passion and so on.

## GEMINI OIL

4 drops Lavender
1 drop Peppermint
1 drop Lemongrass
1 drop Sweet Pea Bouquet

Wear as a personal oil to increase your own powers.

## HEALING OIL

4 drops Rosemary
2 drops Juniper
1 drop Sandalwood

Wear to speed healing.

## HEALING OIL #2

3 drops Eucalyptus
1 drop Niaouli
1 drop Palmarosa
1 drop Spearmint

Another like the above.

### HECATE OIL

3 drops Myrrh
2 drops Cypress
1 drop Patchouly
1 dried Mint leaf

Mix the essential oils in a base of sesame oil. Add the dried mint leaf to the blend. Wear during rituals of defensive magic. Also wear during the Waning Moon in honor of Hecate, Goddess of the Fading Crescent.

### INITIATION OIL

3 drops Frankincense
3 drops Myrrh
1 drop Sandalwood

Use for mystic initiation ceremonies and also to increase your awareness of the spiritual realm.

### INTERVIEW OIL

4 drops Ylang-Ylang
3 drops Lavender
1 drop Rose

Wear to interviews of all kinds to calm you. Helps make a favorable impression.

### JUPITER OIL (PLANETARY)

3 drops Oakmoss Bouquet
1 drop Clove
1 drop Tonka Bouquet

Wear for wealth, prosperity, help in legal matters and all other Jupiterian influences.

### LEO OIL

3 drops Petitgrain
1 drop Orange
1 drop Lime

Wear as a personal oil to increase your own powers.

### LIBRA OIL

4 drops Rose Geranium
2 drops Ylang-Ylang
2 drops Palmarosa
          or
1 drop Rose absolute or otto
1 drop Cardamom

Wear as a personal oil to increase your own powers.

### LOVE OIL

7 drops Palmarosa
5 drops Ylang-Ylang
1 drop Ginger
2 drops Rosemary
1 drop Cardamom

Wear to draw love. Anoint pink candles and burn while visualizing.

### LUNAR OIL

4 parts Sandalwood
2 parts Camphor
1 part Lemon

Wear to invoke the Goddess within.

### MARS OIL (PLANETARY)

2 drops Ginger
2 drops Basil
1 drop Black Pepper

Wear for physical power, lust, magical energy and all Martian influences.

## MERCURY OIL (PLANETARY)

4 drops Lavender
2 drops Eucalyptus
1 drop Peppermint

Wear to draw Mercurial influences, such as communication, intelligence, travel and so on.

## MOON OIL

1 drop Jasmine
1 drop Sandalwood

Wear to induce psychic dreams, to speed healing, to facilitate sleep, to increase fertility and for all other Lunar influences. Also wear at the time of the Full Moon to attune with its vibrations.

## PAN OIL

3 drops Patchouly
2 drops Juniper
1 drop Pine
1 drop Oakmoss Bouquet
1 drop Cedarwood

Wear to be infused with the spirit of Pan. Ideal for magical or ritual dancing, music-making, singing and so on. Also for attuning with the Earth.

## PEACE OIL

3 drops Ylang-Ylang
3 drops Lavender
2 drops Camomile
1 drop Rose absolute or otto

Wear when nervous or upset to calm you down. Stand before a mirror, and while looking into your eyes, anoint your body.

### PISCES OIL

3 drops Ylang-Ylang
3 drops Sandalwood
1 drop Jasmine

Wear as a personal oil to increase your own powers.

### POWER OIL

4 drops Orange
1 drop Ginger
1 drop Pine

To infuse yourself with additional power during potent rituals, anoint with Power Oil.

### PROTECTION OIL

5 drops Petitgrain
5 drops Black Pepper

Wear for protection against all kinds of attacks. Also anoint windows, doors and other parts of the house to guard it.

### PROTECTION OIL #2

4 drops Basil
3 drops Geranium
2 drops Pine
1 drop Vetivert

Another like the last.

### PSYCHIC OIL

5 drops Lemongrass
1 drop Yarrow

Wear to increase psychic powers, especially when working with rune stones, quartz crystal spheres and other such tools.

### PURIFICATION OIL

4 drops Frankincense
3 drops Myrrh
1 drop Sandalwood

Add to the bath or wear to be rid of negativity.

### PURIFICATION OIL # 2

4 drops Eucalyptus
2 drops Camphor
1 drop Lemon

Another like the last.

### SABBAT OIL

3 drops Frankincense
2 drops Myrrh
2 drops Sandalwood
1 drop Orange
1 drop Lemon

Add to an olive-oil base and wear to Wiccan Sabbats.

### SABBAT OIL #2

2 drops Pine
1 drop Ginger
1 drop Cinnamon
1 drop Sandalwood

Add to any base oil. Another like the above.

### SABBAT OIL #3

1 tsp. Frankincense, powdered
1 tsp. Myrrh, powdered
1 tsp. Benzoin, powdered

Add to 1/4 cup olive oil. Heat slowly over low flame until the gums have melted into the oil. Cool and apply sparingly as you would any oil for the Wiccan Sabbats.

### SACRED OIL

3 drops Frankincense
2 drops Sandalwood
1 drop Cinnamon

Anoint your body prior to religious rituals to stimulate spirituality. Also, anoint others during mystical and religious group rites.

### SAGITTARIUS OIL

4 drops Rosemary
2 drops Oakmoss Bouquet
1 drop Clove

Wear as a personal oil to increase your powers.

### SATURN OIL (PLANETARY)

4 drops Cypress
2 drops Patchouly
1 drop Myrrh

Wear to break negative habits, when looking for a house, to create an aura of mystery around you, when going antiquing to find bargains, or for any Saturnian-type rituals.

### SCORPIO OIL

3 drops Pine
2 drops Cardamom
1 drop Black Pepper

Wear as a personal oil to increase your powers.

### SEXUAL ENERGY OIL

2 drops Ginger
2 drops Patchouly
1 drop Cardamom
1 drop Sandalwood

Wear to attract sexual partners. And please, safe sex!

### SLEEP OIL

2 drops Rose
1 drop Mace

Anoint the temples, neck, pulses of both wrists, soles of the feet. It brings on natural sleep.

### SLEEP OIL (DELUXE)

2 drops Rose
1 drop Jasmine
1 drop Camomile

Use as the above.

### SUN OIL

4 drops Frankincense
2 drops Cinnamon
1 drop Petitgrain
1 drop Rosemary

For healing, vitality, strength, promotions and all Solar influences.

### SUN OIL #2

1 tsp. Cinnamon, ground
1 tsp. Juniper berries, mashed
1 Bay leaf, crumpled
a scant pinch genuine Saffron

Gently heat over low flame in 1/4 cup base oil. Strain and use for the above purposes.

### TAURUS OIL

4 drops Oakmoss Bouquet
2 drops Cardamom
1 drop Ylang-Ylang

Wear as a personal oil to increase your powers.

## TEMPLE OIL

4 drops Frankincense
2 drops Rosemary
1 drop Bay
1 drop Sandalwood

Wear during religious rites, those designed to promote spirituality, "temple workings" and so on.

## VENUS OIL (PLANETARY)

3 drops Ylang-Ylang
2 drops Geranium
1 drop Cardamom
1 drop Camomile

Wear to attract love and friendships, to promote beauty, and for other Venusian influences.

## VIRGO OIL

4 drops Oakmoss Bouquet
2 drops Patchouly
1 drop Cypress

Wear as a personal oil to increase your powers.

## VISIONS OIL

4 drops Lemongrass
2 drops Bay
1 drop Nutmeg

Anoint the forehead to produce psychic awareness.

## WATER OIL (ELEMENTAL)

3 drops Palmarosa
2 drops Ylang-Ylang
1 drop Jasmine

Wear to promote love, healing, psychic awareness, purification and so on.

WEALTH OIL

4 drops Tonka Bouquet
1 drop Vetivert

Wear to attract wealth in all forms. Also anoint candles and burn while visualizing.

### End Note:

Those who have read the earlier edition of this book will note many changes in these oil recipes. In fact, I've changed virtually all of them for this new edition to include only true essential oils and a few bouquets.

Folk magicians have always had to invest in tools. Crystals, candles and herbs are three examples. True essential oils, despite their higher prices, are also an investment, but a necessary one for the satisfactory practice of folk magic.

# Ointments

WHEN THE SUBJECT of Witches' ointments is mentioned, the infamous "flying ointments" immediately come to mind, at least to those with some interest in the history of Witchcraft and magic. These salves, consisting of psychoactive plants steeped in a fatty base, were rubbed onto the skin to aid in what is known today as astral projection.

These are not the only types of ointments known to Witches and magicians, however. Many others have more earthly uses that correlate to those of oils. In fact, any of the oils mentioned in the preceding section can be converted to ointments simply by adding them to melted beeswax, lard or (in today's world) vegetable shortening.

However made, ointments should ideally be kept in crystal or porcelain containers. Realistically, any jars with tight-fitting lids will do fine. Keep ointments away from heat and light.

Be warned—though most of the ointments discussed in this section are fairly innocuous, some of them are poisonous and may be lethal. By including them in this work, I'm in no way advocating the use of such hazardous mixtures. These ointments form a part of the herb magic of long-gone days, and so are included here solely for their historical interest.

After the first edition of this book was published, I received many letters from readers who were searching for henbane, hemlock and other baneful herbs. They had obviously ignored my warnings and were intending to make a flying ointment. Needless to say, I didn't help them out—or into an early grave.

Some folks, it seems, won't listen.

## Making Ointments

Ointments are easily made. They consist simply of herbs or oils and a base. In the past, hog's lard was the preferred base because it was readily available, but vegetable shortening or beeswax produces the best results. The base must be a greasy substance that melts over heat but is solid at room temperature. Some herbalists actually use dinosaur fat (i.e., Vaseline, which is prepared from petroleum)!

There are two basic ways to create magical ointments.

### The Shortening Method

Gently heat four parts shortening over low heat until liquified. Watch that it doesn't burn. Add one part dried herbal mixture, blend with a wooden spoon until thoroughly mixed, and continue heating until the shortening has extracted the scent. You should be able to smell it in the air.

Strain through cheesecloth into a heat-proof container, such as a canning jar. Add one-half teaspoon tincture of benzoin (see Tinctures in this book or buy at a drugstore) to each pint of ointment as a natural preservative. Store in a cool, dark place, such as the refrigerator. Ointments should last for weeks or months. Discard any that turn moldy, and lay in a fresh batch.

### The Beeswax Method

This process creates a more cosmetic ointment without a heavy, greasy feeling. It is best to prepare it with oils rather than herbs, as it is difficult to strain.

If possible, use unbleached beeswax. If not, use what you can find. Chip it with a large, sharp knife so that you can pack it into a measuring cup. Place one-fourth cup or so of beeswax in the top of a double boiler (such as a coffee can set into a larger pot of water). Add about one-fourth cup olive, hazelnut, sesame or some other vegetable oil. Stir with a wooden spoon until the wax has melted into the oil.

Remove from the heat and let cool very slightly, until it has just begun to thicken. (This step is taken so that the hot wax won't evaporate the oils.) Now add the mixed oils to the wax. Stir thoroughly with a wooden spoon and pour into a heat-proof container. Label and store in the usual way.

In the recipes that follow, the recommended method of preparation will be mentioned.

### Empowering Ointments

Once the ointment is made and has cooled in its jar, empower it with its particular magical need. This vital step, remember, directs the energy within the ointment, readying it for your ritual use.

### Using Ointments

Ointments are usually rubbed onto the body to effect various magical changes. As with oils, this is done with visualization and with the knowledge that the ointment will do its work.

## The Recipes

### EXORCISM OINTMENT

3 drops Frankincense
2 drops Peppermint
1 drop Clove
1 drop Pine

Add the oils to the beeswax/oil base. Anoint the body when you feel the need for a strong purification.

### FLYING OINTMENT, NONTOXIC

1 part Dittany of Crete
1 part Cinquefoil
1 part Mugwort
1 part Parsley

Add the herbs to shortening and prepare in the usual way. Anoint the body prior to attempting astral projection.

### FLYING OINTMENT, NONTOXIC #2

2 drops Sandalwood oil
1 drop Jasmine oil
1 drop Benzoin oil
1 drop Mace oil

Add the oils to the beeswax/oil base. Use as the above formula.

### FLYING OINTMENT #1 (*don't even consider using this!*)

Cinquefoil
Parsley
Aconite*
Belladonna*
Hemlock*
Cowbane*

### FLYING OINTMENT #2 (*ditto!*)

Hog's lard
Hashish*
Hemp flowers*
Poppy flowers
Hellebore*

I ain't kidding!

### HEALING OINTMENT

4 drops Cedarwood
2 drops Sandalwood
1 drop Eucalyptus
1 drop Cinnamon

Add to the melted beeswax/oil base, cool, and anoint the body to speed healing as needed. Do not apply to wounds, burns or broken skin!

### HEX-BREAKER OINTMENT

3 parts Galangal
2 parts Ginger root, dried
2 parts Vetivert
1 part Thistle

Steep the herbs in shortening, strain, cool, and anoint the body at night.

## LOVE OINTMENT

4 drops Ylang-Ylang
2 drops Lavender
1 drop Cardamom
1 drop Vanilla extract

Add the oils to the beeswax/oil base. Make in the usual way and anoint the body when looking for love.

## LUST OINTMENT

3 parts Galangal
2 parts Dill
1 part Ginger
1 part Peppermint
1 whole Vanilla bean

Prepare with shortening in the usual way. Anoint the body (but not *too* tender areas).

## MOON GODDESS OINTMENT

5 drops Sandalwood
3 drops Lemon
1 drop Rose

Prepare with the beeswax/oil base. Anoint yourself to attune with the Goddess of the Moon and during Full Moon rituals.

## PROTECTION OINTMENT

2 parts Mallow
2 parts Rosemary
1 part Vervain

Make in the usual way with shortening. Rub onto the body to drive out negative influences and to keep them far from you.

### PSYCHIC POWERS OINTMENT

3 parts Bay
3 parts Star Anise
2 parts Mugwort
1 part Yerba Santa

Make in the usual way with shortening. Anoint the temples, middle of the forehead and back of the neck to improve psychic powers.

### PSYCHIC POWERS OINTMENT #2

3 drops Lemongrass
2 drops Bay
1 Yarrow

Mix with the beeswax/oil base and anoint as with the above formula.

### RICHES OINTMENT

4 drops Patchouly
3 drops Oakmoss Bouquet
1 drop Clove oil
1 drop Basil oil

Make according to the beeswax/oil method and anoint the body and hands daily to attract riches.

### SUN GOD OINTMENT

4 drops Frankincense
3 drops Orange
1 drop Cinnamon

Make according to the beeswax/oil method. Anoint the body to attune with the Solar God, especially on Wiccan Sabbats.

### VISIONS OINTMENT (*caution!*)

Hemp*
Angelica
Kava Kava

Make with shortening. Anoint to produce visions. Substitute star anise for the hemp to have *legal* visions.

### WITCHES' OINTMENT, NONTOXIC

3 parts Vervain
3 parts Sandalwood
2 parts Cinnamon
1 part Carnation petals

Make in the usual way with shortening. Store in a container marked with a pentagram (five-pointed star, one point facing up). Anoint the body prior to Wiccan rituals to become one with the Goddess and God and that which lies beyond them.

### WITCHES' OINTMENT, NONTOXIC #2

3 drops Frankincense
2 drops Myrrh
1 drop Sandalwood
1 drop Orange
1 drop Lemon

Make according to the beeswax/oil method. Use as with the above ointment.

### WITCHES' OINTMENT (*caution!*)

Hemlock*
Poplar
Aconite*
Soot

## YOUTH OINTMENT

4 parts Rosemary
2 parts Rose petals
1 part Anise
1 part Fern
1 part Myrtle

Make with shortening. For preserving or re-attaining youth, stand nude before a full-length mirror at sunrise and lightly anoint your body, visualizing yourself as you would like to be.

# *Inks*

OIL LAMPS FLICKERED in the crudely constructed hut. An aged woman gently took her client's hand. The seer lifted a crystal bottle, and muttering an incantation, spilled a pool of ink into the young man's outstretched palm. As the black spot reflected the dancing flames, she divined his future.

Ink has long been used in magic. Perhaps its most useful application lies in its ability to transform symbols or images of our magical goals into visible form. These pictures are then used as focal points during magical ritual to stir up, program and send forth personal energy. Ink, then, is a tool of magic.

Many secret magical textbooks were carefully culled or transcribed during the Middle Ages and Renaissance. Some of these (a few of which have been published in recent times—see the Bibliography) contained sections devoted to the purification and "exorcism" of inks. The inks were used to draw symbols and signs thought to invoke or banish a horde of potentially dangerous beings. Therefore, it was deemed necessary to properly purify inks prior to their use.

Today the magical uses of ink have mostly been forgotten, though some still cast spells with the likes of pseudo "Bat's Blood Ink." When instructed to "inscribe two hearts and the symbol of Venus in green ink" or to "draw an image of your home," many magicians will grab a ball-point pen and scribble away on lined paper. In so doing they're cheating themselves of total involvement in the ritual. Many of us create incenses and oils—why shouldn't we make inks as well?

The first "ink" was probably charcoal; the first pen, a charred stick. Some proto-human who casually scraped a blackened stick on a rock must have been startled to see a dark line trailing after its point.

This can still be done today, of course. Simply burn a stick or branch until its end is reduced to charcoal—not ash. When cool, use the stick as a natural charcoal pencil to trace an image of your goal. A new char-pen should be created for each ritual. As it burns, and as you draw, visualize your magical need.

Such primeval rites may be sufficient to spark your ability to move and direct personal power. If not, try creating your own magical inks.

All magical inks require the use of sharpened quills or dip pens, the latter usually available at stationery and office supply shops. Practice using the dip pen to gain sufficient proficiency before using it for magic.

Two recipes have been preserved from ancient times for magical inks. Unfortunately, they're difficult to make and may not produce satisfactory results. Purely for curiosity's sake, here they are:

## MAGICAL INK #1

10 oz. Gall nuts
3 oz. Green Copperas
3 oz. Rock Alum or Gum Arabic

Reduce all ingredients to a powder and place in a newly glazed earthen pot with river water. Make a fire of sprigs of fern gathered on St. John's Eve (Midsummer) and vine twigs cut on the Full Moon in March. Add virgin paper to this fire and set the pot over it. When the water boils, the ink will be made.

## MAGICAL INK #2

Frankincense "smoke"
Myrrh "smoke"
Rose Water
Sweet Wine
Gum Arabic

Take the smoke of frankincense and myrrh (presumably obtained by holding a spoon over the smoldering gums—see the section on lampblack below). Mix this in a basin with a little rose water and sweet-smelling wine. Add enough gum arabic to make the mixture thick enough to write with.

Such recipes, which date from the 1600s or even earlier, are perfect examples of why magical ink-making has died out. A more simplified version of the second recipe actually does produce a useable ink for those willing to invest time and work in the project. It is printed below.

### Lampblack

Lampblack is used in both the previous and following formulas. It is obtained through the use of a candle. If you're making ink for general magical needs, use a white candle. Inks created for specific goals call for colored candles. For instance, if you're creating an ink for money, use a green candle; for love, a pink taper (see Appendix 1: Colors).

Light a candle of the proper color and hold the back of the spoon's bowl in its flame, barely touching the wick. After leaving it there for, say, 30 to 45 seconds, the flame will have covered the spoon with a black coating. Remove the spoon from the flame and hold it over a small bowl. Carefully scrape off the lampblack into the bowl using a small piece of cardboard or cardstock, such as a three-by-five-inch card.

Ensure that the lampblack actually does fall into the bowl. It's lighter than air and will happily fly all over the table or carpet if you don't watch it carefully.

Repeat this process 30 to 60 times (which will take from 30 minutes to an hour) until you've acquired a generous amount of the flimsy, dark black soot. If you're making an ink for a specific magical goal, visualize it constantly throughout the lampblack gathering.

Your hands will be dirty by this time, and hopefully, the spoon handle won't be too hot.

(If for some reason you're trying Magical Ink #2, collect the soot from smoldering frankincense and myrrh.)

Then make the following recipe. No amounts are given in this formula because lampblack is difficult (impossible!) to measure. One warning though—the longer you collect lampblack, the less miniscule the amount of resultant ink.

MAGICAL INK #3
___

Lampblack
Distilled Water
Gum Arabic

To the bowl of lampblack add warm or hot distilled water *one drop at a time.* Stop adding water before you think you should. Mix the soot and water with a finger until the soot has completely dissolved and the water is inky black. This isn't easy, as lampblack likes to float on top of the water.

If you've added too much water (i.e., if the water is a dull grey), add more lampblack until the dense hue is achieved.

Next, add a small amount of ground gum arabic, and mix with your finger (or a spoon if making a large quantity) until the gum has been dissolved in the warm liquid. The mixture should be as thick as commercially prepared ink. Study a bottle of ink to determine its correct thickness.

Judging the proper proportions of lampblack, water and gum arabic is difficult, but if you follow these instructions you should produce useable magical ink on your first try. After mixing, store in a small bottle and wash your hands—they'll need it.

### Simple Magical Inks

Many of these were included in the previous edition of this book. Try out a few if you wish. If the liquid is too thin to write with, add a bit of gum arabic.

MAGICAL INK #4
___

Saffron essence makes a fine magical ink, but the price is exorbitant.

MAGICAL INK #5
___

Fresh pokeberries, when crushed, produce a purple ink. In fact, one of the names of poke is "inkberry." The seeds are poisonous, so as usual, keep this ink out of your mouth.

MAGICAL INK #6
___

Beet juice makes a reddish ink. Add gum arabic to thicken if necessary.

## MAGICAL INK #7

Try blackberry, boysenberry or grape juice.

## MAGICAL INK #8

"Invisible" inks are easily made, as any Boy Scout knows. Milk, lemon juice and so on are all used, written with a clean dip pen on white paper. This is useful in many types of spells; use your imagination. To make the invisible writing appear, hold the paper carefully over a candle flame (close enough so that the flame heats the paper but doesn't burn it) until the writing appears.

An example of the ritual uses of invisible inks: Write or draw an image of your magical goal with invisible ink. Do this with power, with visualization. When it has dried, stare at the paper and see— nothing. This represents your life without your need. Next, hold it near the candle flame, and as the image slowly appears, send energy into it knowing that the need will manifest in your life as well.

### Using Magical Inks

It's simple. Here are a few ideas:

• Write or draw an image of your magical goal on a piece of appropriately colored paper. Visualize the letters glowing with energy as you write them, or the picture shimmering with power.

• Anoint the paper with oils in harmony with your need and burn it to ashes. As it burns, see the energy you've poured into it streaming out to manifest your need.

• Create a low-cost scrying tool: At night, burn a psychism-inducing incense. Add several drops of black ink to a small, round bowl of water. When the water has darkened, turn off the lights, light a yellow or white candle and gaze into the water. Relax your conscious, doubting mind and allow yourself to contact your psychic mind. Open yourself to receiving information relating to possible future trends.

NOTE: Some old spells call for ink to be taken internally. This may entail drawing an image on a piece of paper, dissolving this in water and downing the liquid. Most commercially prepared inks are poisonous, as are many home-prepared ones, so *do not drink or eat ink!* Keep modern knowledge in mind when performing old rituals.

# *Tinctures*

OILS ARE WIDELY used in magic to stimulate ritual conscious-ness through our sense of smell, as well as to add their own energies to spells. The scented liquids known as tinctures are just as effective as oils. In magical perfumery, a tincture is created by soaking dried plant materials in alcohol, which captures the odor. This process is fairly quick and easy, and creates wonderful products that can be used much as oils are in magic.

However, there is a problem. The alcohol used in magical tinc-turing is *ethyl alcohol*, also known as ethanol or grain alcohol. Iso-propyl, or rubbing alcohol, is distilled from petroleum products; its sharp odor makes it unsuitable for capturing fragrances, so don't try to use it. Ethyl alcohol is a completely natural product distilled from grain, sugar or grapes.

Unfortunately, ethyl alcohol is sometimes difficult to find. It is usually expensive. While "Everclear," a 192-proof alcohol, is some-times available in the United States, it is quite costly. (192-proof alcohol indicates that it contains 96 percent alcohol.) Since I live near the U.S.–Mexican border, I usually buy my ethyl alcohol in Tijuana. Adults are allowed to bring one quart of liquor across the border.

For tincturing you need an alcohol of at least 70 percent strength, or 140 proof. Vodka, which is pure ethyl alcohol, is only 90 proof, or 45 percent alcohol, so it isn't strong enough to produce the best scent. Check liquor stores, supermarkets and drug stores for sources of ethyl alcohol. Once you've found it, you're ready to start making magical tinctures.

The process is almost unbelievably easy. Begin with a good sup-ply of dried plant materials. Fresh herbs won't work due to their water content. Some plants aren't soluble in alcohol—that is, their scents won't transfer to the ethyl and so won't produce highly scented tinctures. Consult the list of recommended herbs in this section or experiment on your own.

Most sources say to use 70 percent alcohol, but I've had good results with 96 percent. If you wish to be adventurous (and also to stretch your alcohol supply), dilute the ethyl with distilled water. This will help capture certain plant scents that aren't fully soluble in water.

### Creating Tinctures

Grind the dried herbs that are to be tinctured in your mortar and pestle. Reduce to the finest possible powder. This is especially important with woods such as sandalwood; you may wish to consider buying them pre-ground.

Next, empower the herb, keeping in mind the magical goal of the tincture you're about to make. Pour the herb into a small bottle with a tight-fitting lid. Using a small funnel, pour just enough ethyl alcohol into the bottle to wet and cover the herb. Cap tightly. Shake the bottle vigorously every day for a week or two. Every time you shake, visualize the tincture's magical goal.

Then, using a coffee filter (or a piece of cheesecloth laid in a strainer), strain the alcohol. The scent may be strong enough at this point—it usually is with gums such as frankincense and myrrh. If not, add more herb to the bottle and pour the alcohol over it. Do this quickly; alcohol evaporates when exposed to air.

Let this sit again and repeat the process, shaking every day. The alcohol should become heavily scented and colored. (In fact, this may happen soon after you add the alcohol to the herbs.) If it doesn't you're using a plant that isn't readily soluble in alcohol. Add a bit of water to the alcohol and try again, or select one of those herbs mentioned in this section.

To correctly determine whether the tincture is properly scented, apply a drop or two to your wrist. Wait until the alcohol has evaporated and then sniff. Many tinctures won't smell "true" in the bottle.

When the plant's scent has completely overpowered the sickly-sweet alcohol odor, filter it one last time, bottle, add a few drops of castor oil or glycerine to stabilize the fragrance, and label and store in a cool place out of direct sunlight until needed.

Now that you've made your magical tincture, what do you do with it?

## Using Tinctures

*Under no circumstances drink a magical tincture!* Many of the plant materials used in magical tincturing can be harmful if swallowed. The 192-proof alcohol certainly isn't very healthy for you, either.

However, there are other uses. One of these was mentioned in the Incense section: scented incense papers. This seems to work best with gum and resin tinctures or with any heavily fragranced tinctures.

Some tinctures can be used to anoint the skin, to bring the plant's power within you, but try this out on a small area of the skin at first. The alcohol will quickly evaporate, leaving the plant's scent. Some tinctures can be irritating to the skin, while others leave rather nasty stains or gummy, sticky residues. This is often the case with frankincense and copal tinctures. Lavender, clove, patchouly and many other tinctures are fine for anointing purposes, but all alcohol-based tinctures can dry sensitive skin.

Tinctures can also be used to anoint magical tools, sachets, candles and jewelry; added to bath water; mixed in with oils; added to ointments and so on. Virtually all ritual uses of oils also apply to tinctures.

Following are some herbs that I've tinctured with good results. Also included are some sample recipes for you to try. You may find, as I have, that tincturing is far more reliable in capturing certain plants' scents than is any other do-it-yourself method.

A few quick notes: ethyl alcohol will quickly "take" scents from such spices as clove and star anise. Gums such as frankincense, myrrh, benzoin and copal also work well, though the results, as mentioned above, can be rather gummy. Other herbs are rather hit-and-miss affairs. Experiment!

## Recommended Tincturing Materials

BENZOIN—This dark brown, translucent tincture is cleanly antiseptic-smelling, and is perfect for increasing business success and sharpening mental powers. It is used in purificatory rituals such as anointing and then burning a white candle. A few drops of benzoin tincture can be added to scented oils and to ointments to preserve them.

CAMPHOR—Use only real camphor, of course. This produces a clear tincture with a penetrating, cool odor. Sniff it to lessen sexual desire. Use it to anoint healing amulets (sachets) or add to Full Moon baths.

CINNAMON—A gorgeous, rich scent. Anoint money sachets, add to money baths, sniff to develop psychic powers, add to protective blends. The tincture is a deep red, almost brownish black hue.

CLOVE—Another incredible scent. Use in protection and exorcism formulas. Anoint money with clove tincture before spending. Use for love. Makes a transparent, light brown tincture.

COPAL—This fine gum from Mexico produces a light yellow, translucent tincture that feels tacky on the skin. Its scent is reminiscent of a combination of frankincense and lemon. Anoint for protection and use in spirituality formulas.

DEERSTONGUE—A warm vanilla scent. Sniff to increase psychic powers. The light green tincture is also used to attract men.

FRANKINCENSE—One of the first tinctures I ever made, frankincense produces a beautiful golden-colored tincture with a full frankincense scent. Once you've smelled this, you'll realize that most frankincense oil is purely synthetic. Anoint tools, sachets or the body (if you don't mind sticky skin). Use for spirituality, exorcism, purification, luck and protection rites. This is one of the best tinctures to use in scenting incense papers.

GALANGAL—This rootstock produces a light yellow tincture smelling of ginger and camphor. Use for luck, money, protection, exorcism and psychic development.

LAVENDER—This light green tincture can be used to attract love; to produce sleep by anointing your forehead and pillow; to purify by adding to baths, and to promote chastity and peace.

MYRRH—A bittersweet brown tincture. Myrrh is used for spirituality, healing and protection purposes. The scent recalls ancient times and is evocative when mixed with frankincense. Another tincture well suited for use with incense papers.

NUTMEG—A translucent, reddish-orange tincture. Sniff to increase psychic powers, or anoint money, health and luck amulets (sachets).

PATCHOULY—This heady, earth-scented herb makes an evocative green tincture. It is useful for money, love and fertility purposes.

PEPPERMINT—Though slow-going, the results are worth your efforts. This mint-green tincture is used in money, purification and love rituals. Anoint sleep pillows. Try spearmint, too.

ROSEMARY—A rich, resinous tincture, yellowish green in color. It can be used for nearly every magical goal: love, healing, protection, exorcism, sleep, lust and so on.

SAGE—I use the local white sage for this tincture, which produces a powerful, greenish-brown tincture. Its scent is somewhat similar to camphor with a strong "green note." It is used in healing, purification, obtaining wisdom and protection, and can also be used to anoint wishing amulets or sachets.

SANDALWOOD—This is another herb that is slow to tincture. Be sure to use *ground* sandalwood for this and give it a try. This tincture seems to take the longest to "cook," but when finished, smells like sandalwood with a slight cedary odor. Use for protection, spirituality, healing and exorcistic purposes.

STAR ANISE—This spicy, star-shaped herb produces a sassafras-smelling tincture. Sniff to improve psychic awareness, especially before working with tarot cards, rune stones and other divinatory tools.

TONKA—A rich vanilla scent with a slightly bitter after-note. Anoint money, love, courage and wish amulets (sachets), but do not take internally. Tonka beans are poisonous and, therefore, are becoming harder to obtain.

VANILLA—This familiar culinary herb makes a rich, warm-smelling tincture. It is useful to attract love, to promote physical energy, and to stimulate mental processing.

WOOD ALOE—This Malaysian bark produces a tincture smelling of ginger and pepper, highly resinous. It is perfect for anointing sacred tools, the altar, luck and spirituality amulets and talismans.

To reiterate: Don't sniff tinctures until after the alcohol has evaporated from them—after anointing. Once the alcohol evaporates, the herb's scent will blossom before your nose.

The above list is short, but it is a good starting point for those interested in magical tincturing.

Following are a few formulas for tinctures that you can try. They are combinations of some of the herbs mentioned above. All of these are safe for anointing on the skin, but their alcohol content does make them drying. Gum-based resins, again, can be sticky. (Don't say I haven't warned you!)

For proportions, use equal parts unless your psychic awareness tells you otherwise. Mix them exactly as you would oils.

Remember that when using tinctures (as with all magical herb products), do so with visualization and power.

## The Recipes

### GUARDIAN TINCTURE

Cinnamon
Sandalwood
Clove

Anoint yourself or objects for protection.

### HEALTHY MIND, HEALTHY BODY TINCTURE

Sage
Myrrh
Rosemary

Anoint your body, healing amulets (sachets), blue candles and so on to speed healing or to retain good health.

## LOVE TINCTURE

Lavender
Rosemary
Patchouly

Anoint your body or love sachets to attract a love and to expand your ability to give and to receive love.

## MONEY TINCTURE

Patchouly
Clove
Nutmeg
Cinnamon

Anoint money before spending; anoint money amulets, your purse or wallet, cash register and so on.

## SACRED TINCTURE

Frankincense
Myrrh
Benzoin

Anoint yourself to increase your involvement with spiritual activities, especially prior to meditation and religious rituals of all kinds.

## THIRD EYE TINCTURE

Star Anise
Clove
Nutmeg
Deerstongue

Anoint your pillow for psychic dreams (careful though; this will probably stain—use one pillowcase just for this purpose). Also anoint the wrists and forehead before using your natural psychic abilities.

# Herb Baths

A BAG OF HERBS rests in a tub of warm water. As they soak, the plants emit tinted, scented water. The magical bath begins.

Adding herbs to the bath is certainly one of the easiest forms of magic. In essence, a tub of water containing a bath sachet is little more than a huge pot of herb tea in which the bather brews. When herbs are placed in warm water they release their energies as well as their scents and colors. As such, baths are powerful tools in gaining psychic awareness, drawing love, speeding healing and granting personal protection.

## Making the Sachets

Choose to follow one of the recipes included in this section, or create your own. Each bath mixture may be prepared in advance and saved until needed if kept in an airtight jar.

Once you've assembled all ingredients, add them to your mixing bowl. Mingle the herbs with your fingers, pouring your power into them and visualizing your magical goal. When mixed, place about a handful or so in the center of a large square of cheesecloth. Tie up the ends and add this to the bath. If you don't have any cheesecloth, simply use an old washcloth.

To save time in the future, make up several bath sachets. Place them in a jar with a tight-fitting lid and store.

## Using the Sachets

This is simple. Fill the clean tub with warm water. Place the sachet in the tub and let it steep until the water is colored and scented.

If you don't have a bathtub, or if you simply prefer showers, make up a sachet in a washcloth and scrub your body with this after your normal shower, just before toweling.

A third method of utilizing the sachets is a bit more complicated. Heat two cups water until boiling. Pour this over one or two sachets in a heat-proof container. Cover and let the herbs steep for ten to thirteen minutes. Remove the sachets, squeeze out the last drops of scented water from them, and pour the infusion into the bath.

Some natural magicians prefer to add the flowers, herbs and barks directly to the water without first enclosing them in cloth. This is almost certain to leave you with petal-covered skin and clogged plumbing if you don't spend ten minutes or so picking herbs out of the water after your bath.

As you step into the tub, feel the herb's energies mixing with your own. Visualize your magical goal. Don't make the herbs do all the work—invite their energies inside you and send them out to the universe (through your visualization) to bring your need into manifestation. Repeat the bath for as many days as you feel is necessary.

I've had people write to me asking how long they should repeat magical baths. There are no rules in this area. As I just said, continue the baths until you feel that they've done their work. That's it!

If you wish, burn an appropriate incense and perhaps some candles in the bathroom while you soak.

## *The Recipes*

### ANTI-HEX BATH

4 parts Rosemary
3 parts Juniper
2 parts Bay
1 part Mugwort

Soak in this mixture at night to purify you of all ills.

## APHRODISIAC BATH

3 parts Rose petals
2 parts Rosemary
2 parts Thyme
1 part Myrtle
1 part Jasmine flowers
1 part Acacia flowers

Add three drops of musk oil to the tub. Bathe before meeting a lover, or bathe with a friend!

## BEAUTY BATH

3 parts Lavender
3 parts Rosemary
2 parts Spearmint
1 part Comfrey root
1 part Thyme

Place a hand mirror next to the tub. Lie back, smell the scented water, and close your eyes. Relax. Be at peace. Visualize yourself as you wish to appear, then open your eyes. Hold the mirror before your face and see the new you.

## "BREAK THE HABIT" BATH

2 parts Rosemary
1 part Lavender
1 part Lemongrass
1 part Lemon Verbena
1 part Sage

To rid yourself of negative, baneful habits as well as their root causes: Place the sachet in the tub. After it has colored the water, step into it. Lie back in the water and visualize yourself happily avoiding the habit or other negative condition—smoking, drinking, drugs, depressions, obsessions and so on. Visualize the water absorbing your desire and need for the habit. See in your mind's eye all the energy you've been giving to this negative condition seeping out into the water. When you've visualized all that you can, pull the plug and sit in the tub until the water has drained out. Splash fresh water onto your body, washing away all traces of the taint. Repeat daily.

### DIETER'S MAGICAL BATH

2 parts Rosemary
2 parts Fennel
1 part Lavender
1 pinch Kelp

For best results, repeat this bath morning and night. While in the tub, visualize yourself as possessing complete control over your eating habits. See yourself eating sensible foods in sensible quantities. For symbolic associations, begin this bath regime two days after the Full Moon and continue until the New Moon. On the last day of the two-week period, visualize yourself as you wish to be—slim, fit, healthy.

### DIVINATION BATH

3 parts Thyme
2 parts Yarrow
2 parts Rose
1 part Patchouly
1 part Nutmeg

Bathe in this mixture directly before practicing any form of divination, to relax the conscious mind and to stimulate psychic awareness.

### ENERGY BATH

3 parts Carnation
2 parts Lavender
2 parts Rosemary
2 parts Basil

Use when fatigued or depressed. Gives a lift, especially if you let the water cool slightly before bathing. Visualize the water sparkling with fiery droplets of energy that melt into your body, lending you vitality and power.

### EXORCISM BATH

2 parts Basil
2 parts Rosemary
1 part Yarrow
1 part Cumin
1 pinch Rue

Bathe in this mixture to cleanse yourself of negativity, especially when you feel that someone (or some*thing*) is out to get you. Visualize the energy-packed water absorbing the negative energies from your body. Splash fresh water over your body after this bath to remove all traces of the negativity.

### HEALING BATH

3 parts Rosemary
2 parts Lavender
2 parts Rose
1 part Peppermint
1 part Cinnamon

To be used, of course, in conjunction with conventional medical attention. This bath speeds the healing process. To help shake off a cold, add two parts eucalyptus to this formula. (Avoid bathing if your doctor so informs you.)

### LOVE BATH

3 parts Rose petals
2 parts Lovage
1 part Dill

Bathe in this mixture daily to bring a love into your life. Visualize yourself as a loving, caring person seeking another of like mind.

### LOVE BATH #2

3 parts Rose petals
2 parts Rose Geranium
1 part Rosemary

Another like the above.

## LOVE BATH #3

3 parts Orange flowers
2 parts Lavender
1 part Gardenia petals
1 part Cardamom
1 part Ginger
1 part Rosemary
1 part Rose petals

A third like the above.

## MONEY BATH

3 parts Patchouly
2 parts Basil
1 part Cinnamon
1 part Cedar

Bathe in this mixture to increase your finances.

## MONEY BATH #2

3 parts Clove
2 parts Cinnamon
1 part Galangal

Another like the above.

## PEACE BATH

2 parts Catnip
2 parts Hops
1 part Jasmine
1 part Elder flowers

Bathe to stem anger and to relieve stress. Visualize yourself releasing the anger or stress into the water as you sit in it. Feel it floating out and the water absorbing the hurt, pain, nerves and wrathful feelings. Splash fresh water onto your body after the bath.

## PROTECTION BATH

4 parts Rosemary
3 parts Bay
2 parts Basil
2 parts Fennel
1 part Dill

To strengthen your psychic armor, bathe in this mixture daily until you feel strong.

## PSYCHIC BATH

3 parts Lemongrass
2 parts Thyme
2 parts Orange peel
1 part Clove
1 part Cinnamon

Use before working with your psychic awareness. Or, repeat this bath daily to become increasingly aware of psychic impulses. Visualize.

## RITUAL PURIFICATION BATH

4 parts Lavender
4 parts Rosemary
3 parts Thyme
3 parts Basil
2 parts Fennel
2 parts Hyssop
1 part Mint
1 part Vervain
1 pinch Valerian root

This recipe, adapted from *The Key of Solomon*, is ideal for use before all types of magical rituals, or when you simply wish to feel clean and free of impurities. If you add more than a pinch of valerian, you'll be sorry. It smells—well, trust me; it smells!

## SUMMER MAGICAL CLEANSING BATH

3 parts Marjoram
3 parts Thyme

Use this mixture during the spring and summer to wash away the chills of winter and to "spring clean" yourself.

## WINTER MAGICAL CLEANSING BATH

3 parts Pine needles
2 parts Bay
1 part Rosemary

Bathe in this blend during the winter months to refresh and revitalize your magical energies.

## WITCH'S BATH

3 parts Rosemary
3 parts Carnation petals
2 parts Galangal
2 parts Cinnamon
1 part Ginger

While bathing in this mixture, visualize yourself possessing perfected abilities to rouse, direct and release personal power. Use prior to all types of positive magical rituals for extra potency.

# Bath Salts

BATH SALTS ARE an easily prepared alternative to bath herbs, and are to be preferred to the caustic mixtures now on the market. Most of these chemical-ridden formulas are almost guaranteed to irritate your skin.

## Creating Bath Salts

The basic ingredients are table salt, baking soda (sodium bicarbonate) and Epsom salts (magnesium sulfate). Some herbalists also use borax. Add the salts to a large bowl in these proportions:

3 parts Epsom salts
2 parts baking soda
1 part table salt (or Borax)

Mix thoroughly. This is now the base from which you can create a wide variety of bath salts. With this you can make up a large quantity of one type of bath salt. If two or three types are preferred, simply divide the base and set aside those portions to be separately fragranced and colored.

It's wise to add the power of colors to bath salts. Use plain food coloring for this purpose, letting it fall drop by drop onto the salt base. If two or more colors are required to mix an exotic hue (such as purple), mix these in a spoon first and then add to the salts to avoid creating a two-toned product. Recommended colors for all bath salt mixtures are included in the recipes. For those that read "Color: White," simply leave them untinted.

Add many drops for a darker colored salt; fewer for a lightly hued salt. Mix the color into the salts with a spoon until it is evenly distributed.

Now add the essential oils drop by drop, one ingredient at a time, until the scent seems right. Mix with a spoon until all salt particles are moistened. Be prepared to spend some time doing this, perhaps a half hour or so. As you mix, visualize the energies within the oils merging with each other and with the salt. Keep the salt's magical goal in mind while you stir.

Empower the mixture according to the basic ritual in Chapter 3. Use or store until needed.

As to proportions: Though each recipe lists relative proportions (two parts almond oil; one part mint), rely on your nose to determine the exact quantities (such as one tablespoon or 30 drops). The more potent the finished product's scent, the less will have to be used for each bath. Bath salts should be strongly scented.

To use, add from two tablespoons to one-half cup of the ritual bath salts to a full tub. Mix with your hands, feeling their energies merge with the water.

While sitting in the tub, soak up the power. Allow yourself to receive it, or alternately, to release specific negative energies from yourself into the water.

Directly after every ritual bath (and before, if necessary), clean your tub, either with a commercial cleanser or with a damp cloth covered with baking soda. Ritual baths taken in unclean bathtubs won't have the desired effects!

The proportions here, though for essential oils, are by parts. One part may equal six drops. Generally speaking, there shouldn't be more than ten total drops of essential oil per half-cup of bath salts. Experiment to find what works best, and please use only genuine essential oils.

# The Recipes

### AIR BATH (ELEMENTAL)

3 parts Lavender
2 parts Rosemary
1 part Peppermint
1 part Bergamot Mint Bouquet
Color: Yellow

Use to attune with the powers of Air, for divination, theorization, aiding the memory, concentration, clear thinking, visualization and study.

### CELIBACY BATH

4 parts Lavender
2 parts Camphor
Color: White

Add to a tub of tepid water—not hot. Bathe in this blend when you wish to cool down.

### CIRCLE BATH

3 parts Rosemary
2 parts Myrrh
2 parts Sandalwood
1 part Frankincense
Color: Purple

Bathe in Circle Bath before any form of magical working to strengthen, purify and prepare yourself for ritual.

### EARTH BATH (ELEMENTAL)

4 parts Patchouly
3 parts Cypress
1 part Vetivert
Color: Green

For use in attuning with the Earth, or for spells involving money, foundation, stability, creativity, fertility, ecology and so on.

### EXORCISM BATH

3 parts Frankincense
3 parts Sandalwood
2 parts Rosemary
1 *drop* Clove
Color: White

Bathe in this mixture for a heavy psychic cleansing. Splash fresh water over your body after the bath. NOTE: Do not add more than one drop of clove essential oil—it can irritate the skin.

### FIRE BATH (ELEMENTAL)

3 parts Frankincense
2 parts Basil
2 parts Juniper
1/2 part Orange
Color: Red

For use in attuning with the element of Fire, or for rituals involving strength, courage, passion, lust and so on.

### FLOWERY LOVE BATH

3 parts Palmarosa
2 parts Lavender
1 drop Rose
Color: Pink

Bathe in this mixture to attract love and to expand your ability to give and to receive love. NOTE: I've specified one drop of rose because of its high cost. More can be added if desired; indeed, rose absolute can be used in place of palmarosa, which is much less expensive.

### HEALING BATH

3 parts Niaouli
2 parts Eucalyptus
1 part Sandalwood
Color: Dark Blue

For use in speeding healing. Release the ailment into the water. Splash fresh water over your body before toweling. And don't bathe, of course, if your condition doesn't allow it.

### HIGH AWARENESS BATH

3 parts Cedarwood
2 parts Sandalwood
1 part Frankincense
Color: Purple

Bathe in this mixture to direct your consciousness toward higher things, to promote spirituality and to combat Earth-obsessions such as uncontrolled spending, overeating, sluggishness and all forms of unbalanced materialism.

## LOVE BATH

3 parts Rosemary
2 parts Lavender
1 part Cardamom
1 part Yarrow
Color: Pink

For promoting and attracting love. Use with visualization, as with all of these formulas.

## LUST BATH

3 parts Sandalwood
2 parts Patchouly
1 part Cardamom
Color: Red

For promoting lustful desires.

## PROTECTION BATH

3 parts Rosemary
2 parts Frankincense
1 part Lavender
Color: White

Bathe in this mixture daily to strengthen your psychic armor and to stave off all manner of attacks—physical, mental, spiritual, psychic and emotional.

## PSYCHIC BATH

4 parts Yarrow
1 part Bay
Color: Light Blue

Use this blend in baths to strengthen your psychic awareness.

## PURIFICATION BATH

3 parts Geranium
2 parts Rosemary
1 part Frankincense

Bathe in this blend to purify body, spirit and soul.

## SEA WITCH BATH

3 parts Lotus Bouquet
2 parts Lavender
1 part Rosemary
Color: Dark Blue

Add a bit of sea salt to the salt base. Bathe in Sea Witch Bath for a gentle purification prior to magical works.

## SPIRITUAL BATH

4 parts Sandalwood
2 parts Myrrh
1 part Frankincense
1 *drop* Cinnamon
Color: Purple

Use to increase your awareness of the divine, especially before religious rituals. NOTE: Use only one *drop* of cinnamon essential oil.

## WATER BATH (ELEMENTAL)

2 parts Camomile
2 parts Yarrow
1 part Ylang-Ylang
1 part Palmarosa
Color: Dark Blue

Use for attuning with the element of Water, or for love, psychic awareness, friendships, healing and so on.

## WATER BATH (ELEMENTAL) #2
### (a less expensive version)

2 parts Palmarosa
1 part Sandalwood
1 part Myrrh
1 part Geranium
Color: Dark Blue

Another like the last.

# Brews

MIDNIGHT. LIGHTNING SLASHES the stormy sky. Three haggard figures on a lonely hill lean over a huge cauldron. They throw noisome ingredients into the boiling water—poisonous herbs, noxious reptiles, snake venom—and cackle as steam rises and the wind howls like tortured demons.

So goes the standard brew-making scene, thanks in large part to authors such as William Shakespeare. They vividly captured and firmly implanted such powerful but absurd images in our minds.

Brews (also known as potions) may be as prosaic as herb tea, or as mystical as rainbow infusion. They stem from early magical, ritual and medicinal preparations, and are as effective today as they were thousands of years ago.

In herb magic, brews are little more than herbal infusions or teas. They needn't be prepared over an open fire in a forest clearing; your own stove or backyard will do nicely.

The brews in this chapter answer a variety of needs and are utilized in various ways. Some are drunk, others added to the bath, and still others prepared to release fragrant steam into the air, infusing the area with the sum total of the herb's vibrations.

## It's the Water

The type of water used in brewing is of some importance. Well, spring and distilled waters are preferred over that which pours from the tap. You can buy these bottled or collect them from the source, so long as it's unpolluted and free running. Rain water is ideal for use— except when gathered in smoggy areas. Tap water can be used as a last resort, but consider purchasing the bottled variety in the future.

In the last edition of this book I mentioned that distilled water is used for medicinal preparations, "which is fine, but *not* for magical operations, for it is inert." Why this change of heart? If you're going to drink the brew (or even if you're not), distilled water is definitely better than chlorinated, fluoridated, bacteria-filled tap water. If it's all you have, use it.

Sea water and mineral water aren't recommended due to their high mineral content.

## Brewing

### The Heating

Fire, gas flame or stove coils will do for the heat source. I suppose you could prepare a brew in a microwave oven, but this isn't the best idea. If nothing else, it reduces some of the *magic* of the process.

If you're the old-fashioned kind, try making a brew in a fireplace or outdoors over a blaze.

### The Vessels

It's best if the water and herbs don't come into direct contact with metal while brewing. There are few exceptions to this in herbalism. One is cauldron brewing, which is little-practiced today. Herbal products prepared with double boilers may also require metal pots. But in general, avoid metal.

Clear glass jars work well for Solar infusions. Simply place the water and herbs into the jar and set this in direct sunlight, preferably outdoors. Leave it there for most of the day. Some brews included here are made with glass jars of various colors.

### The Brew

Not every brew included in this section is made in the following manner; use specific instructions where given.

For a basic brew: Gather, grind and mix the herbs. For brews to be drunk, use a separate culinary mortar and pestle for grinding, not the one used for heavy-duty magical herbs.

Empower the herbs with your magical goal.

Heat about two cups water to boiling. Place about one handful of mixed, empowered herbs in a teapot or some other heat-proof, non-metallic container. Pour the water over the herbs. Cover with an equally nonmetallic, steam-tight lid. Let the herbs brew for about 13 minutes. Strain through cheesecloth or a bamboo strainer, and use as directed.

Brews should be used as quickly as possible. If necessary, they can be stored in the refrigerator for three or four days. After this time return them to the Earth and create a new brew.

A note regarding "love" potions. There are no drinks that will emotionally enslave another person to you, no brews that will cause love. However, some brews have long been celebrated for relaxing inhibitions and mellowing the emotions. Also, a few have been used to smooth over difficulties during long-term relationships and marriages. A few of these are included here, but they're definitely not love potions!

## *The Recipes*

### APHRODISIA: A PASSION DRINK

1 pinch Rosemary
2 pinches Thyme
2 tsp. Black Tea
1 pinch Coriander
3 fresh Mint leaves (or 1/2 tsp. dried)
5 fresh Rosebud petals (or 1 tsp. dried)
5 fresh Lemon tree leaves (or 1 tsp. dried Lemon peel)
3 pinches Nutmeg
3 pieces Orange peel

Place all ingredients into teapot. Boil three cups or so of water and add to the pot. Sweeten with honey, if desired. Serve hot.

### APHRODISIA #2

5 parts Rose petals
1 part Clove
1 part Nutmeg
1 part Lavender
1 part Ginger

Make in the usual way, preferably in an earthen pot. Add this mixture to tea, or serve alone to increase the passions.

### CAULDRON OF CERRIDWEN BREW (*caution!*)

Acorns*
Barley
Honey
Ivy*
Hellebore*
Bay

Boil water in a cauldron over an open fire. Place all ingredients into the cauldron. Sit before it and entrance yourself by watching the flames. Smell its mystic scent and receive wisdom. (*Do not drink. Why? It's poisonous, that's why!*)

### CAULDRON OF CERRIDWEN BREW (nontoxic)

1 part Bay
1 part Tobacco
1 part Damiana
1 part Mormon Tea
1 part Broom

Use according to the above directions.

### CLAIRVOYANCE BREW

3 parts Rose petals
1 part Cinnamon
1 part Nutmeg
1 part Bay
I part Mugwort

Place in teapot, fill with boiling water, let steep, covered, for a few minutes. Remove cover, sniff steam (not so that you burn your nose) for a few moments, visualize the mystic scent opening your psychic awareness, then lie down and prophesize. If you wish, drink a bit of the brew as well, and let the steam continue to rise as you stretch your psychic awareness.

## DREAM TEA

2 parts Rose petals
1 part Mugwort
1 part Peppermint
1 part Jasmine flowers
1/2 part Cinnamon

Mix, add one teaspoon to a cup. Pour boiling water over this and let steep, covered, for a few minutes. Drink before going to bed to produce psychic dreams.

## EXORCISM BREW (*caution!*)

3 parts Rosemary
1 part Bay
1 pinch Cayenne*

Mix, add one teaspoon mixture to a cup, pour boiling over the herbs and let steep for nine minutes, covered. Drink a few teaspoons a day, or add to the bath.

(Cayenne pepper is marked here with a *caution!* because it is a strong herb. Use with care and respect.)

## ISIS HEALING BREW

1 part Rosemary
1 part Sage
1 part Thyme
1 part Cinnamon

Half fill a blue-glass bottle with fresh water. Add the ground, empowered herbs to it and let this sit in the Sun all day. If by sunset the water has been colored by the herbs, it is ready for use. If not, store in the refrigerator overnight and steep in the Sun the following day. Strain. Anoint the body or add to bath water while visualizing yourself as being in perfect health.

## KERNUNNOS PROTECTION BREW

1 part Pine needles
1 part Caraway
1 part Bay
1 part Basil
1 part Anise

In a red-glass bottle half-filled with water, steep the herbs in the Sun for a day. Strain and add to bath water, or anoint your body for personal protection. Also, anoint protective amulets and talismans.

## LOVE WINE

3 tsp. Cinnamon
3 tsp. Ginger
1 one-inch piece Vanilla bean
2 cups Red Wine
2 tsp. Rhubarb juice (optional)

Score the vanilla bean along its length. Add herbs to the red wine with the vanilla bean. Add two teaspoons rhubarb juice (if available), and let sit for three days. Serve.

## MONEY BREW

3 parts Sassafras
2 parts Cedar
1 part Allspice
1 part Clove
1 part Dill
1 part Vetivert
1 part Calamus

Half fill a green-glass bottle with fresh water. Add about a handful or so of the mixed, empowered herbs. Cap tightly and leave in full sunlight all day. At dusk, sniff the water. If the scent is strong, strain and add to baths, wash hands, anoint money charms and so on. If it isn't strong enough, chill overnight and return to the Sun the following day.

### MOON BREW

Set a silver container filled with water out on the night of the Full Moon just as it rises (which will be at sunset). Allow the water to soak up Lunar rays all night. Just before dawn, rise and retrieve the water. Place in an earthen jug and cork tightly. (Never expose to the rays of the Sun.) Add to the bath for love; anoint money to increase wealth; touch to the brow to promote psychic awareness; place in the bath to attune with the spiritual planes or prior to Lunar rituals.

### PROTECTION BREW (*caution!*)

3 parts Rue
2 parts Rosemary
1 part Vetivert
1 part Hyssop
1 part Mistletoe*

Brew as usual, strain and anoint each window and door of the house. Pour the rest down the drains to safeguard them. *Do not drink!*

### PSYCHIC TEA

3 parts Rose petals
2 parts Yarrow
1 part Cinnamon

Brew, strain and drink a cup before or during divination and psychic work to enhance your psychic awareness.

### PURIFICATION BREW

Collect any nine sacred plants, such as vervain, rue, rosemary, oak, pine, acacia, rose, carnation, thyme, basil, jasmine and so on. Place in a nonmetallic pot or bowl. Add rain water (or fresh water) and let the herbs soak, covered and away from light, for three days. Strain. Use for asperging the house, others, or yourself for purification. (See A Miscellany of Recipes for instructions on creating aspergers.)

## PURIFICATION BREW #2

1 part Lemon Verbena
1 part dried Lemon peel
1 part Camomile

Brew, drink for purification prior to ritual. If desired, add a splash of lemon juice, a teaspoon of honey or sugar. (Sugar is used by Peruvian shamans in purification ceremonies.)

## RAINBOW BREW

When it rains, wait for the clouds to break somewhere and look for a rainbow. If you find one, put a saucer or some other nonmetallic pan outside where it can catch rain. If it rains while the rainbow is still present, save the water for ritual uses. It has been blessed by the rainbow's appearance. Because the rainbow contains all colors, this "brew" is useful for all types of magic. Bottle and label. Add to baths or anoint the body and hands while visualizing your magical goal.

## SLEEP BREW

1 part Rose petals
1 part Myrtle leaves
1 part Vervain

Soak rose petals in a pot of water for three days. Add more rose petals each day. On the third day, add myrtle and vervain at sunrise and let soak all day. That night, just before going to bed, bathe your forehead with three handfuls of the brew. Your sleep should be free from nightmares. Use the brew until gone, then make another batch if needed.

## SOLAR CLEANSING BREW

2 parts Fern
2 parts Juniper
2 parts Rosemary
1 part Cumin
1 part Yarrow
1 part Pepper
1 part Rue

Place the ground, mixed and empowered herbs in a red bottle half-filled with water. Set this in the Sun, let steep, strain. For a gentle cleansing, sprinkle the brew around the house at sunrise for three or four days every month.

## SUN WATER

Set a glass or crystal container of pure water outside just at dawn, in a place where the Sun's rays will shine on it all day. At sunset, bottle and cork the water. Keep it in a sunny place. Add to baths for energy, sprinkle around the home to remove evil, anoint yourself for purification and so on.

# Ritual Soaps

BY THE LIGHT of a candle's flame, you're lying in a tub of herb-scented water, preparing yourself for magic. Incense smoke drifts on the air as you form a perfect mental image of your magical goal. Steam rises, laden with the fragrance and energies of flowers, seeds, roots and leaves.

Then, nearing the end of your bath, you reach for the soap—and it's sickly sweet, artificially perfumed. Your concentration is destroyed, pulling your attention from your ritual preparations.

Has this happened to you? It has to me. Although soaping isn't necessary in magical baths, a ritually correct soap can be a boost to any spell's effectiveness. Even if you don't bathe before ritual, it is wise to wash your hands. Even such a minor purification ritual can trigger the state of ritual consciousness. Therefore, spell soaps would be ideal for such uses.

Where can we obtain them? Don't try the supermarket. Make them at home. Not many people know how to do this today, but it's a lot of fun.

Most commercial soaps are formulated with caustic chemicals. They can be quite irritating to the skin, and are usually obnoxiously perfumed. Ritual soaps (of varying quality) are occasionally available at occult stores, but why not try making your own?

Don't worry—you won't have to get a fire crackling under your cauldron out in the countryside to do this. And unless you want to upset your neighbors with nasty smells and risk burning your hands with lye, it's best to start out with pure, natural castile soaps. These can be purchased at most drugstores and markets. Oils or herb brews are then added to the soap. The magic is in the scent and in your empowerment of the soaps.

Pure castile soap is usually made of coconut oil. Kirk's, a coconut castile made in the Phillipines, is ideal. Castile soap (named after Castile, Spain) is also made from olive oil, but I haven't had good results using this variety.

Any castile soap can be drying to the skin. If you have problems in this area, try adding one to two teaspoons apricot, almond or coconut oil to the water prior to mixing (see the below recipes), reducing the amount of water accordingly.

There are two types of ritual soaps: sphere and liquid. Here are complete directions for creating both forms.

### Ritual Soap Spheres

Using a very sharp, thick-bladed knife, cut a four-ounce bar of castile soap into very small pieces no larger than 1/4-inch square—the smaller (so long as they're cubes) the better. Place these in a heat-proof nonmetallic container.

Heat slightly less than 1/3 cup water until nearly boiling. Pour the still-hot water over the cut-up soap. Let it sit until the water has cooled sufficiently to allow you to handle it. Mix the soap and water with your hands. This will moisten the soap chips, but they shouldn't be floating on the surface of the water. If they are, add more soap.

Let the soap and water sit for about nine minutes until mushy. If the soap cubes are still hard, set the bowl in a pan of water and reheat it gently until the soap is soft.

While the soap is melting, mix together the oils and empower them with your magical need. Then add 20–50 drops of the combined oils to the soap/water mixture. Very warm water evaporates the oils, so wait until the water has cooled. Mix them in thoroughly. The scent should be strong; if not, add more oils.

The quality and strength of the oils you use determines the quantity needed to overpower the natural, rather antiseptic scent of genuine castile soap. Just add them until you can smell the oils.

Divide the scented soap mass into three or four parts. Form these into spheres with your hands. Place each on a nine-inch-square piece of cotton cheesecloth. Pull the ends tightly around the sphere, gather them at the top and twist together. The cloth should be tightly wrapped around the soap sphere. Tie the ends closed with strong string. Repeat with each sphere.

Hang the soap spheres in a warm place for three days, or until the soap is completely hard. When the spheres won't give to finger pressure, remove the cloth wraps. The soaps are ready to be used in ritual baths. Or, they can be wrapped in clean cheesecloth, labelled, and given as gifts to friends who would appreciate them.

## Liquid Ritual Soap #1

Liquid soaps are a new trend today, thanks to aggressive advertising by major manufacturers. These soaps, however, are actually detergents, and aren't the best substances to put onto your hands.

While ad agencies trumpet liquid soaps as if they were brandnew, the idea is actually as old as soap. American Indians agitated yucca and other suds-producing plants in water to create cleansing solutions. Ancient Hawaiians used the flowers of a wild ginger plant for the same purpose. Many saponin (soap-producing) plants grow throughout the world and were often the only source of soap for various peoples.

But we'll use castile as the basis of liquid ritual soaps. Here's the method:

Grate castile soap into a large bowl. Pack this into a measuring cup until you have exactly one cup. Remember to pack that soap!

Heat three cups water until almost boiling. Add the soap chips to the water. Turn off the heat and whip with a wooden or (if you have nothing else) metal whisk until the soap is completely melted.

Let sit until cool, then add 50–60 drops of the mixed, empowered oils. Once again, the exact amounts vary. You'll know it's time to stop adding oils when the soap is heavily scented.

Using a funnel, place the liquid soap in a jar. Cap and shake vigorously to mix in the oils. Label and use as needed.

## Liquid Ritual Soap #2

You can also try making liquid spell soaps with brews. To the three cups hot water add five to six tablespoons mixed, dried, ground and empowered herbs rather than the oils mentioned in the following recipes. Take off the heat, let steep for 10 to 13 minutes and strain. Gently reheat the water, add one cup castile soap shavings, whisk and allow to cool. It is ready for use.

Unfortunately, when herb brews are mixed with castile soap the scent changes dramatically. If you try it, you'll understand what I mean. If you don't like the results, fortify the scent with a few drops of the oil form of one of the included herbs.

To use liquid soaps, simply wet your hands and apply a few drops of the soap. It foams easily and leaves your skin clean and scented.

The recipes follow. As you can see, there are endless varieties of soaps waiting to be concocted. Most of the oil recipes in this book can be used in scenting soaps. Once you've mastered the basics, make up a few types and keep them on hand in case of ritual need.

Some of these recipes suggest using rose water or orange flower water in place of plain water in making the soap/water mixture. This can be used or not, but use only water scented with genuine orange flower essential oil or rose essential oil.

Store unused soaps in your altar if it is designed with cupboards or shelves below it. Or, simply place them in your herb cupboard.

Remember—use ritual soaps *with power*. Visualize your magical goal as you wash.

## *The Recipes*

### ISIS SOAP

3 parts Myrrh
2 parts Frankincense
1 part Lotus Bouquet

Use before any Egyptian or Isian ritual. Also, wash with this soap to develop spiritual awareness. If you wish, substitute rose water for the water in which the soap chips are melted.

## LOVE SOAP

4 parts Geranium
3 parts Palmarosa
2 parts Neroli
1 part Ginger

Wash with this soap to attract love, or prior to love rituals. And again, rose water may be used in the same proportions as plain water in preparing the soap.

## LUCK SOAP

2 parts Vetivert
1 part Orange
1 part Nutmeg

Wash to change your "luck" or to bring positive energies into your life. Orange flower water may be used in place of plain water during soap manipulation.

## MONEY SOAP

3 parts Patchouly
2 parts Peppermint
1 part Basil
1 part Pine
1 part Cinnamon

Wash your hands daily with this soap to attract money, or use prior to money-drawing rituals.

## MOON SOAP

3 parts Sandalwood
2 parts Camphor
1 part Lemon
1 part Eucalyptus

Use before rituals on the Full Moon to attune with its energies.

### PROTECTION SOAP

4 parts Rosemary
3 parts Basil
1 part Frankincense
1 part Bay
1 part Mint

Wash daily with this soap when you feel the need for protection, or before such spells.

### PSYCHIC SOAP

3 parts Lemongrass
2 parts Bay
1 part Cinnamon

Wash with this soap to increase your psychic awareness, especially prior to divinatory or psychic workings.

### SABBAT SOAP

| | |
|---|---|
| 4 parts Sandalwood | 1 part Myrrh |
| 3 parts Rosemary | 1 part Bay |
| 2 parts Patchouly | 1 part Lemon |
| 1 part Cinnamon | 1 part Ginger |

Use during ritual baths prior to the Sabbats (see Glossary) or as a general magical cleanser.

### WITCH'S SOAP

3 parts Rosemary
2 parts Pine
1 part Cinnamon
1 part Orange

Wash with this soap before rituals of all kinds to increase your personal power.

# Sachets or Herbal Charms

MAGICAL SACHETS—ALSO known as herbal charms (or amulets and talismans)—consist of herbs and other materials tied up in bits of cloth.

Some sachets ward off certain energies and disease; others draw specific situations or powers to you. In this new edition I've included astrological sachets for use by those wishing to stress the positive aspects of their Sun sign. They can be worn every day as a personal power booster or placed on the altar to magically represent you.

Sachets are easily made and have a long history. Cloth hasn't always been used. Herbs have been carried in horns, seashells, leather, fur and lockets. Magical rings were made into sachets by placing an appropriate herb below the jewel. Thus, the energies of both gem and herb worked toward the magical goal. Herbs were also sewn into clothing for protective purposes.

### Creating Sachets

For most sachets, a handful or less of the empowered herb mixture is more than enough, depending on its desired size. Household sachets tend to be larger than ones designed to be carried on the person.

First, mix the herbs. Empower them with your magical need. *Know* that the herbs are pulsating with specific, programmed energies that are being released toward your goal.

Next, select the properly colored cloth. Choose a natural fiber material such as felt, wool or cotton. Synthetic materials such as polyester seem to disturb the herb's frequencies. Cut the cloth into a square from four to nine inches across. Place the empowered herbs on the center of the cloth, gather up the ends and tie them firmly together. You've trapped the herbs within the cloth. Use a natural cord such as wool yarn or cotton twine to shut the sachet.

A large stock of yarn and cloth in a wide array of colors is helpful. Felt works well and is available in many shades.

## Using Sachets

If it is a personal charm, hold it in your hand, squeeze it gently to release its fragrance, and carry with you at all times.

If the sachet is designed for the house or car, squeeze and place it in the most appropriate spot.

Replace with freshly made sachets every three months or so, disassembling and burying the old ones.

## The Recipes

### ANTI-SORCERY SACHET

1 part Dill seed
1 part Flax seed
1 part Peony root

Tie up in white cloth, wear or carry, suspend over doors and windows.

### ANTI-SORCERY SACHET #2

1 part Trefoil (Clover)
1 part Vervain
1 part St. John's Wort
1 part Dill

Tie up in white cloth and wear. To guard your home, hang in a window.

## ANTI-THEFT SACHET

2 parts Rosemary
1 part Juniper
1 part Caraway seeds
1 part Elder
1 pinch Garlic

Tie up in white cloth and hang over the front door to protect the home and its contents. If you don't enjoy the strong garlic odor, use a pinch of crumbled garlic skins.

## ANTI-TOOTHACHE SACHET

1 tbsp. Salt
1 Bread crumb
1 small piece Coal

Tie up in a piece of red silk and carry when pains begin. See a dentist to ensure that the sachet works!

## AQUARIUS SACHET

3 parts Lavender
2 parts Patchouly
1 part Benzoin
1 part Mace
1 part Mint

Mix, tie up in gray or some other dark-colored cloth that appeals to you. Wear or carry to strengthen the positive aspects of your sign.

## ARIES SACHET

3 parts Carnation
2 parts Juniper
1 part Frankincense
1 part Fennel
1 part Cumin

Blend the empowered herbs, tie up in red cloth and wear or carry to strengthen the positive aspects of your sign.

## CANCER SACHET (MOONCHILDREN)

3 parts Sandalwood
2 parts Myrrh
1 part Gardenia
1 part Lemon Balm
1 part Gardenia petals

Tie up in white cloth and carry with you to strengthen the positive aspects of your sign.

## CAPRICORN SACHET

3 parts Vetivert
2 parts Cypress
1 part Vervain
1 part Mimosa blossoms
1 part Comfrey

Mix, tie up in indigo, gray or any other dark cloth you prefer. Wear or carry to enhance the positive aspects of your sign.

## CAR PROTECTION SACHET

2 parts Rosemary
2 parts Juniper
1 part Mugwort
1 part Comfrey
1 part Caraway
1 small Quartz Crystal point

Tie up in red cloth. Secrete somewhere in the car where it won't be found. And drive safely—this sachet won't guard against the driver's mistakes.* After a few months, take the sachet apart, save and cleanse the crystal (using Crystal Purification Incense, perhaps) and use again in the new sachet.

---

*See *The Magical Household* for more car protection rituals.

## CAR PROTECTION SACHET #2

3 parts Rosemary
2 parts Juniper
2 parts Basil
1 part Fennel
1 part Mugwort
1 part Vervain
1 pinch Salt

Another like the above.

## GAMES OF CHANCE SACHET

3 parts Patchouly
2 parts Nutmeg
1 part Jasmine flowers
1 part Cloves
1 part Cinquefoil
1 small Lodestone

Tie up the empowered herbs in green cloth and carry with you when risking your money for possible future return—investments, gambling, speculation.

## GEMINI SACHET

3 parts Lavender
2 parts Mint
2 parts Gum Mastic
2 parts Clover
1 part Dill seed
1 part Anise

Tie up in yellow cloth and carry with you to enhance the positive aspects of your sign.

## HEALING SACHET

2 parts Cinnamon
2 parts Sandalwood
1 part Rose petals
1 part Cayenne
1 part Ginger
1 part Rue

Mix, tie up in blue or purple cloth. Anoint sachet with Eucalyptus oil and wear or place near the bed at night.

## HOME PROTECTION SACHET

3 parts Rosemary
3 parts Basil
2 parts Fennel seed
2 parts Dill seed
1 part Bay
1 part Fern
1 pinch Salt

Tie up in red cloth. Situate the sachet in the highest place inside the home.

## HOME PROTECTION SACHET #2

1 part Fleabane
1 part St. John's Wort
1 part Capers (dry them before using)
a few grains Whole Wheat

This formula, from ancient Middle Eastern magic, should be tied up in red cloth and hung over the front door.

### LEO SACHET

2 parts Orange peel
2 parts Cinnamon
1 part Frankincense
1 part Nutmeg
1 part Juniper
1 pinch Gum Arabic

Tie up in orange, gold or red cloth and carry with you to enhance the positive aspects of your sign.

### LIBRA SACHET

2 parts Spearmint
2 parts Catnip
2 parts Rose petals
1 part Marjoram
1 part Thyme
1 part Mugwort

Tie up in yellow cloth and carry with you to enhance the positive aspects of your sign.

### LOVE SACHET

3 parts Lavender
2 parts Rose petals
1 part Orris root

Tie up in pink cloth. Place the sachet among your clothing to infuse it with the scent of love. Or, wear to attract a love.

### LOVE SACHET #2

3 parts Rose petals
2 parts Orange flowers
1 part Jasmine flowers
1 part Gardenia flowers

Another like the above.

## LOVE "SPECIAL" SACHET

4 parts Rose petals
1 part Orange peel
1/2 part Carnation petals
1 pinch Baby's Breath

Mix, tie up in pink cloth and wear.

## MONEY SACHET

3 parts Patchouly
2 parts Clove
1 part Oakmoss
1 part Cinnamon

Tie up in green cloth and carry to attract money.

## NIGHTMARE CURE (*caution!*)

1 part Lupine
1 part Helenium (Heliotrope or Sunflower)
1 part Marshmallow
1 part Dock
1 part Elder
1 part Wormwood
1 part Strawberry leaves
1 part Yew berries*

Tie up in light blue or white cloth. Hang on bedpost near your head. This ancient formula also cures "water elf disease," as well as mischief caused by goblins! No guarantees are made for this formula's effectiveness.

## PISCES AMULET

3 parts Sandalwood
2 parts Sage
1 part Eucalyptus
1 part Anise
1 part Lemon

Tie up in a purple cloth and wear or carry to enhance the positive aspects of your sign.

## PROTECTIVE SACHET

3 parts Dill seed
2 parts Caraway seed
1 part Flax seed
1 pinch Salt

Tie up in white or red cloth and carry for protection.

## PROTECTIVE SACHET #2

2 parts Marjoram
1 part Angelica root
1 part Dill seed
1 part Clove

Tie up in white cloth; place in a window.

## SACRED BUNDLE SACHET

3 parts Cachana root
1 dried Chile pepper
1 kernel Corn
1 pinch powdered Turquoise

Wrap in white cloth and bury near your front door (or in a flowerpot) to guard your home and to bless it with power.

## SAGITTARIUS SACHET

3 parts Sassafras
2 parts Cedar
2 parts Clove
1 part Star Anise
1 part Dragon's Blood
1 part Juniper

Tie up in purple cloth and wear or carry to strengthen the positive aspects of your sign.

## SCORPIO SACHET

3 parts Pine
3 parts Myrrh
2 parts Galangal
1 part Allspice
1 part Violet flowers
1 part Basil

Tie up in bright red (or blue, if you prefer) cloth. Wear or carry to strengthen the positive aspects of your sign.

## SPICY ROSE SACHET

1 part Rose—for love
1 part Rosemary—for remembrance
1 part Hibiscus—for delicate beauty
1 part Clove—for dignity
1 part Camomile—for energy in adversity

Tie up in pink cloth and give to one you love.

## TAURUS SACHET

3 parts Patchouly
2 parts Oakmoss
1 part Cardamom
1 part Rose petals
1 Vanilla bean, crushed

Tie up in yellow or blue cloth and wear or carry to strengthen the positive aspects of your sign.

## TRAVEL PROTECTION SACHET

1 part Mustard seed
1 part Comfrey
1 part Irish Moss
1 part Bladderwrack (also known as Kelp)

Tie up in white or yellow cloth. Carry with you when travelling, and tuck one into each suitcase and garment bag as well.

### TWELVE-HERB YULE SACHET

| | |
|---|---|
| 7 parts Juniper | 2 parts Rosemary |
| 4 parts Cinnamon | 2 parts Lemon peel |
| 4 parts Allspice | 2 parts Orange peel |
| 4 parts Ginger | 1 part Clove |
| 4 parts Caraway | 1 part Bay |
| 2 parts Nutmeg | 2 pinches Orris root |

Tie up in green or red cloth and give as gifts on Yule or Samhain.

### VIRGO SACHET

3 parts Lavender
2 parts Patchouly
2 parts Cypress
1 part Caraway
1 part Fern
1 part Mint

Tie up in a clear yellow cloth and wear or carry to enhance the positive aspects of your sign.

### WEALTH SACHET

2 parts Cinnamon
2 parts Lemon Balm
1 part Cinquefoil
1 part Clove
1 whole Vanilla bean
1 whole Tonka bean

Crush the vanilla bean and mix all together. Empower. Tie up in purple or green cloth. Carry to increase riches and to establish a positive cash flow.

## WEATHER PROTECTON SACHET (*caution!*)

1 part Mistletoe*
1 part Cedar
1 part Broom
1 part Bryony

Tie up in white cloth and hang near the chimney, in the attic, or elsewhere high in the house to protect it and its occupants against the ravages of the weather.

## WITCH-FINDER TALISMAN

1 part Rue
1 part Agrimony
1 part Maidenhair fern
1 part Broomstraw
1 part Ground Ivy

Tie up in purple cloth and wear to know other Witches, if you are lonely and seek others of the Old Ways.

# *Powders*

POWDERS HAVE LONG been an integral part of folk magic. They consist of ground herbs which are sprinkled to release their powers. A powder is an incense never burned, a sachet never worn.

I included two powder recipes in the last edition of this book (in Chapter 12: A Miscellany of Recipes), and devoted a portion of the video *Herb Magic* to this subject as well. I've also used them sporadically over the years. Still, I questioned the necessity of including this section.

After reviewing this expanded edition, I realized that the 10 distinct types of magical compounds already discussed, not to mention the hundreds of recipes, were bordering on overkill. Just how many forms of herb magic is anyone willing to practice, or at least, read about?

But I decided that if this book hoped to be a complete introduction to magical perfumery, a section on powders was necessary. Additionally, many of the ritual uses of powders are unique to this form. Hence, this section.

## *Making Powders*

Simply grind herbs as finely as possible. To save time you can buy ground herbs, but doing so cheats you of really getting in touch with them.

While mortaring the herbs, during the whole long process, visualize . . . imagine . . . *see* your magical goal. Perhaps I haven't emphasized the need for *empowering* herbal products often enough in this book. To reiterate, the power lies within herbs and within ourselves. If we don't empower powders, incense or oils, if we don't accurately "program" them with our magical goals through visualization and concentration, such mixtures will have only slight effects. If you forget the empowerment, you might as well forget the magic!

Now that I've stepped down from my soapbox—once the herbs are powdered, mix them together. Empower them and the powder is ready for use.

### Using Magical Powders

The easiest method is to simply scatter them when and where you need their energies. Other methods are also available:

• Sprinkle the powder in a circle around you, beginning and ending in the East and moving clockwise. Sit within this circle and absorb the powder's energies.

• Those who work with crystals and stones can add powders to their rituals. Sprinkle the appropriate powder around the crystal (or crystals) as it lays on the altar to increase its power.

• Sprinkle powders around candles before being burned to boost their energies.

• Scatter a ritually appropriate powder over the altar before spells.

• Sprinkle on the altar in specific shapes to use as focal points for visualization: protection powder in pentagrams; love powder in hearts; psychic powders in circles. It doesn't matter if the powder remains in the shape for long. And so on, as your imagination teaches you.

But remember—do this solely for positive purposes, to affect your possessions, yourself or others from whom you've obtained permission. *All manipulative magic is negative magic and will rebound on the magician.*

One note: some powders, particularly those that contain dragon's blood, will stain carpets, bedsheets, clothing and other materials. Be aware of this when sprinkling.

Happy powdering!

## *The Recipes*

### ASTRAL TRAVEL POWDER

2 parts Sandalwood
1 part Mugwort
1 part Cinnamon

Sprinkle on the bedsheets and pillow before sleeping to encourage consciously directed astral travel.

### EXORCISM POWDER

3 parts Basil
2 parts Frankincense
2 parts Rosemary
1 part Yarrow
1 part Rue

Sprinkle throughout the house, or in any place needing a strong purification and protection.

### HAPPINESS POWDER

2 parts Lavender
1 part Catnip
1 part Marjoram

When you wish to lift your spirits, sprinkle this powder in a circle on the floor or ground and sit within it, drinking in the powder's energies. Visualize them surrounding you and infusing you with joy.

### HEALTH POWDER

2 parts Eucalyptus
1 part Myrrh
1 part Thyme
1 part Allspice

Sprinkle in the sickbed or in the recovery room to speed the body's healing process. Or scatter on the altar and burn blue candles.

## LOVE POWDER

3 parts Yarrow
3 parts Lavender
2 parts Rose petals
1 part Ginger

For use in attracting love. Be sure to sprinkle the bedsheets or bedroom.

## LUCK POWDER

2 parts Vetivert
2 parts Allspice
1 part Nutmeg
1 part Calamus

Use to bring positive changes into your life.

## MONEY POWDER

2 parts Cedar
2 parts Patchouly
1 part Galangal
1 part Ginger

To attract money, sprinkle in your place of business, in your wallet or purse. Rub onto money before spending. Or, sprinkle in a dollar sign on the altar and burn green candles over the symbol.

## PROSPERITY POWDER

3 parts Sassafras
2 parts Cinnamon
1 part Pine

To attract wealth in all its forms.

## PROTECTION POWDER

2 parts Dragon's Blood
2 parts Sandalwood
1 part Salt

Mix and sprinkle outside around your property to dispel and stave off negativity.

## PROTECTION POWDER #2

2 parts Mugwort
2 parts Frankincense
1 part Dill
1 part Juniper
1 part Cumin

Sprinkle where you need protection, inside or out. For personal protection, sprinkle in a circle and stand within it until you're charged with the herb's energies. Do this daily to lend protective energies to yourself at all times.

## PSYCHIC POWDER

2 parts Yarrow
1 part Rose petals
1 part Lemongrass
1 part Eyebright

Sprinkle before exercising your innate psychic awareness.

## SPIRITUALITY POWDER

2 parts Wood Aloe
1 part Frankincense
1 part Myrrh
1 part Sandalwood

Sprinkle in room prior to meditation or religious rituals to turn your awareness to higher things. Also, sprinkle in circles around blue candles for this purpose.

## WISHING POWDER

2 parts Sage
1 part Sandalwood
1 part Tonka

In a lonely place, hold the powder in your right hand (if right-handed). Feel its energies and visualize your wish with perfect clarity. Rouse the power within you and send it into the powder. When it is jumping with energy, fling it as far from you as you can. As the powder touches the Earth, it releases its energy and goes to work to bring your wish into manifestation.

# A Miscellany of Recipes

THESE RECIPES DON'T seem to fit anywhere else, and so have been grouped here under this convenient heading.

## ASPERGER

Mint
Rosemary
Marjoram

Use sprigs of these fresh herbs. Tie the stem-ends together with white thread or string and use to sprinkle brews on yourself, on others or throughout your house. Visualize while utilizing the asperger. Also use for sprinkling salt water around the home to dispel negativity. Aspergers are used in Wiccan and magical ceremonies. Make a fresh asperger for each use.

## ASPERGER #2

Vervain
Periwinkle
Sage
Mint
Ash
Basil

Use sprigs of the fresh plant materials. Tie to a handle of virgin hazelwood (i.e., from a tree that has not yet borne fruit) and use for sprinkling as in the above.

## BALEFIRE (a magical fire)

Cypress
Laurel
Oak

Make a fire of the above woods and branches while visualizing its flames purifying and empowering all those near it. Use for any occasion when meeting with others for magical or ritual rites. It is purificatory and power-enhancing in its effects.

## FRANKINCENSE PROTECTIVE NECKLET

Several ounces of Frankincense "tears"
(small, rounded lumps)

Empower the frankincense tears with protective energies. Thread a short, thin needle with yellow cotton thread. Heat the needle in a gas flame, in hot water or in a candle flame. (If using a candle flame, quickly wipe off the lampblack—if any—that forms on the needle.) Push the hot needle through the center of a frankincense tear and move it down onto the thread. Repeat the heating and threading process until you've created a necklet of frankincense "beads" that you can slip over your head. Knot the ends well and wear for protection or during magical rituals.

## MEXICAN HEALING RUB

1 handful Yellow Daisies
1 handful Violets
1 handful Poppies
1 handful Rosemary

Mix together these fresh plant materials. Empower. Place in a large ceramic bowl. Wet the herbs thoroughly with vodka or some other nonodorous alcohol. If you don't wish to use alcohol, substitute apple cider vinegar. Rub the ill person's body with the wetted herbs, visualizing them absorbing the disease.

When finished, bury the herbs and wash your hands.

## MONEY PENTACLES

4 tbsp. ground Cloves
4 tbsp. ground Cinnamon
4 tbsp. ground Nutmeg
4 tbsp. ground Ginger
a few drops Cinnamon oil
a few drops Clove oil
a few drops Nutmeg oil
2 tbsp. ground Gum Tragacanth (or Gum Arabic)
4 tbsp. Water

Combine the spices. Add the oils to them and mix well. Empower. Add the gum tragacanth to the water and mix thoroughly. Let it sit until it has absorbed the water. Add the ground, empowered spices to the gum/water mixture and blend well with your fingers. This should produce a stiff, dough-like mixture. If the mixture is too mushy, add a bit more of the ground spices. With your hands, form into flat, one-inch circular shapes. Using a sharp knife, trace a pentagram (five-pointed star) onto each flat circle. Let sit in a warm place out of the Sun to dry. When dried to a rock-hard consistency, carry in the pocket or purse to attract money. Or, place on the altar between two green, flaming candles that have been anointed with patchouly or cinnamon oil. If you wish, make a larger pentacle of the spices and ring with green candles to speed money your way. After four weeks bury the pentacle in the Earth with thanks and use a new one.

## PILLOW, ASTRAL TRAVEL

3 parts Mugwort
2 parts Vetivert
1 part Sandalwood
1 part Rose petals
1 Vanilla bean, crushed
1 pinch ground Orris root

Make into a small pillow. Sleep on it to promote astral travel during sleep.

## PILLOW, DREAM

2 parts Rose petals
2 parts Lemon Balm
1 part Costmary
1 part Mint
1 part Clove

Sew up into a small pillow and sleep on it to have vivid dreams.

## PILLOWS, MAGIC

Use each herb individually, or mix for several purposes. Make these pillows small, about five inches square. Set them on top of your regular pillow.

Anise: halts nightmares
Bay: pleasant dreams
Camomile: restful sleep
Eucalyptus: healing
Hops: sleep, healing
Mugwort: dreams, psychic dreams
Peppermint: if used fresh, it induces sleep; replace daily
Thyme: happiness (eases depression)
Verbena: aphrodisiac
Yarrow: dreams of loved ones

## POMANDER LOVE CHARM

1 large, perfect, fresh Orange or Lemon (see below)
2 tbsp. ground Cinnamon
2 tbsp. ground Coriander
2 tbsp. ground Ginger
1 tbsp. ground Orris
Whole Cloves

If you wish to attract a man, use an orange. If a woman, a lemon. Choose a fruit that is free of bruises or discoloration, which is firm and nearly ripe.

Grind the herbs. Place in a small bowl, mix together and empower with your need for love.

Hold the orange or lemon and visualize yourself in a loving relationship. Place an empty bowl or plate below the fruit to catch dripping juice. Push one of the cloves into the fruit. Now, retaining the visualization, push another clove as close as possible to the first one but slightly to one side. Continue adding cloves until you've formed a rough heart shape on the surface of the lemon or orange.

Still visualizing, add more cloves until the orange is completely studded with them. You'll probably get some juice on your hands.

When the fruit is so covered with cloves that little of its skin shows, place it in the bowl of mixed, empowered spices. Roll it in the mixture until it is completely covered with the loving spice mixture. Leave it in the bowl for one to two weeks. Every day or so, roll the pomander over the spice mixture.

After a few weeks remove the pomander. Empower the pomander with your magical need. Place it on your altar. Anoint six pink candles with a love oil such as rose, jasmine, palmarosa or one of the blends suggested in this book. Set the candles in a circle around the pomander. Light the candles and let them flame for nine minutes or so while visualizing yourself in a relationship.

Tie the pomander with a pink cord, string or piece of yarn and hang it up where you'll see it, and smell it several times a day. Let the candles burn out.

The pomander will do its work.

## PURIFICATION BLEND

1/2 cup Apple Cider Vinegar
1 handful fresh Eucalyptus leaves
1 handful fresh Rue leaves
3 pinches Salt
1 quart Water

Add the herbs to the vinegar and let sit overnight. Strain through cheesecloth and add to the water with the salt. Use the mixture to wash objects to be purified, such as jewelry, amulets or magical tools. Or add a half-cup amount to your bath. This is actually a very weak, diluted tincture.

## ROSE LOVE BEADS

1 part fresh Rose Geranium leaves
2 parts fresh Rose petals—the more fragrant the better
Rose Water

Remove the white stem-ends from the rose petals. Empower the fresh herbs with your need for love. Cover the petals and leaves with rose water in a nonmetallic pan. Simmer, covered, for 30 minutes. Ensure that the mixture doesn't actually boil. Turn off the heat and let soak until the next day. Repeat the simmering again for a half hour. Repeat this for three days in all, adding rose water when necessary. On the last day squeeze out all water until you have a fragrant mess. The mixture should be dry enough to hold its shape. Form into small, round beads with your hands, each about 1/4 inch long. Push a large needle or stiff wire through each bead while it's still wet to form holes for stringing. Let dry for a week or so, moving them around to ensure even drying. String on pink thread, yarn or ribbon. The beads are ugly and black, but when worn on the body they release a delicious rose scent. Wear these for love, or add to sachets, place in purses and so on.

## WITCHES' LOVE HONEY

1 cup pure, light Honey
2 broken Cinnamon sticks
1 tsp. whole Cloves
1 dime-sized piece of Sugar Ginger*
1 inch-long piece dried Lemon peel
1 inch-long piece Vanilla bean
1 pinch ground Cardamom

Empower all herbs and the honey with your magical intent. Pour the herbs into a jar with a tight-fitting lid. Add the honey and shake until all herbs are moistened. Cover it tightly with the lid and place the jar on your herbal altar between two pink candles. Light the candles and let them burn out. Let the honey sit in a dark place for three weeks. Add small portions to food and hot beverages to promote good feelings and love.

---

* Look for sugar (or crystallized) ginger in Asian food markets, herb stores and gourmet food shops.

Part III
Substitutions

# *Introduction*

YOU MAY BE ALL set to mix up a batch of incense and then discover that, to your dismay, you're lacking one or two ingredients. Might as well put everything back and wait until you can obtain the proper herbs. Right?

*Wrong!*

The recipes in this book are truly suggestions, examples of mixtures that have proven to be effective. This doesn't mean that you can't alter them to fit your stock at hand, or simply change them to your liking.

If you lack some of the ingredients (wood aloe, for instance, is difficult to obtain today), simply substitute an herb with the same basic energies.

I'm amazed at how many people hesitate to substitute. Here's a slightly exaggerated example of a conversation that I have with alarming regularity:

"Have you got any gum assagraxanathicthon?" Great Herbal Magician asks me.

I snap my fingers. "Fresh out. What're you making?"

"An *ancient* incense for spirit manifestation," Great Herbal Magician says, lifting an eyebrow.

"Hmmm. Why don't you substitute gum mastic or dittany of Crete?"

"No! It *has* to be gum assagraxanathicthon!" G.H.M. huffs. "This 25,000-year-old recipe plainly states that if I don't use gum assagraxanathicthon, *evil spirits* will carry me off to the *Burning Sands of Araby!*" His lower lip trembles.

"Oh, it's for protection. Then you have three choices: substitute asafoetida, don't make that particular recipe—or pack for hot weather."

A far-fetched conversation? Not really. I've spruced it up a bit to make my point: magical recipes needn't be slavishly followed.

Before I get any requests for it, there isn't any "gum assagrax-anathicthon." Nor are there are 25,000-year-old recipes floating around.

*Substitutions are not only encouraged, they're often mandatory.* While most of the ingredients mentioned in this book are available somewhere, at some price, none of us can stock them all. Therefore, anyone who makes up more than a few of these recipes will need to substitute.

Many recipes mentioned in other, more sensationalistic books (such as any of the spurious "Necronomicons" currently in circulation) list unknown, unidentified, long-extinct or nonexistent herbs. These are included for the following reasons:

1. To impress the reader with the author's "scholarship" and access to obscure magical textbooks (many of which are so obscure that they've disappeared).

2. To test both the reader's knowledge of the subject and her or his ability to disregard such false information and to substitute an ingredient with the same properties.

3. Because the author simply didn't know any better.

Therefore, it's impossible to compose some of these recipes without substituting.

True, I've included a few formulas in this book with unknown herbs—*selenetrope* in Moon Incense #2 and *Tapsus barbatus* in Spirit Incense #2. In the first instance I suggested substitutes; the latter recipe isn't recommended for use anyway, and so I have left it intact.

I'm not of the old school to which so many authors seem to belong: "Write to obscure; write to confuse."

So when you're out of sandalwood or come across an empty jar of lavender oil in your cupboard, refer to this section and determine the best substitute. The same is true if you find a recipe somewhere that includes selenetrope, *Tapsus barbatus* or even "gum assagrax-anathicthon," as well as any poisonous substances.

How do you do this? It's best to know the missing ingredient's magical powers. With this in mind you can determine why it has been included in that particular recipe, and can substitute a plant with similar energies.

Even if you're not sure why lemon oil was included in a purification blend, you can at least look under Purification in the tables and find some other oil to use in its place.

A few examples:

Say you're creating a Fast Money Oil composed of mint, patchouly, pine and cinnamon. Then you remember that the last patchouly oil you saw cost $10 a bottle, and you only had a few bucks on you. You decided not to buy any.

So you look at the Money and Riches table in this section and study it, finally deciding on vetivert oil. It has a somewhat similar scent, is ritually appropriate, and you have a bottle on hand. Presto! You've successfully substituted vetivert oil for patchouly oil.

It can be that simple. If you wish to ensure that your substitution is the best possible choice (keeping in mind your in-stock selection of herbs), research each of the possibilities in books. Look at their backgrounds, their basic energies and their recommended magical uses. From this knowledge, choose the most appropriate herb.

When trying to compound formulas found in other sources, many problems can arise. Say you're reading Agrippa's *Three Books of Occult Philosophy*, originally published in English in 1651 (see Bibliography). For some reason you've decided to mix up the "fume," or incense, of Mars. Here are the ingredients—no amounts are given.

> Euphorbium
> Bdellium
> Gum Armoniak
> Roots of both Hellebors
> Loadstone
> a little Sulphur
> Brain of a Cat, or blood of a Bat*

Hmmm. Quite an incense, but for some reason, you decide to try to produce it.

First off, you decide to omit the brain or blood—for, um, *obvious* reasons. Such ingredients were used in earlier days to bind the incense

---

* According to the 1651 English edition. A 1974 edition (see Bibliography) listed this line of ingredients as "the brain of a hart, the blood of a man and the blood of a black cat." This lurid change seems suspicious to me.

together, as well as to add their supposed energies to the completed product.

If you wish to substitute something for the brain or blood, try egg white—an ancient symbol of life and a good binder.

Now, to euphorbium. This is the poisonous, milky juice of any of 4,000 species of the common *Euphorbiaceae* family, which grows worldwide. Perhaps the best-known member is the poinsettia. In ancient times euphorbium (the milky secretion of any species of *Euphorbia*) was used in medicine and magic. Its virulently poisonous nature probably contributed to its inclusion in this recipe.

Not wishing to commit suicide-by-incense, you look at the Mars table in this section for possible substitutes. How about tobacco? Though it's poisonous, adding a pinch of pipe tobacco to an incense won't kill you. Fine. You settle for tobacco.

Now gum bdellium. This is a rare substance gathered from several species of the *Buseraceae* family, which grows in India and Africa. Although known for at least 6,000 years, gum bdellium is virtually unobtainable today.

However, copal, the gum resin which has been used in New World rites since Mayan times, is obtained from a *Bursera* spp. tree. It is—at least distantly—related to gum bdellium. Additionally, gum bdellium is said to have a cedar-like aroma. Some types of copal could, I suppose, be described this way. The fact that both are gums (and that you have two ounces of the stuff in your herb cupboard) seems to indicate that it is a fine substitute. So, copal. You won't find this under the Mars heading but it is acceptable.

Using closely related plant materials is a valuable method of determining substitutions. You don't have any copal? Not to worry. The Mars list includes dragon's blood and pine resin. One of these could be used to replace gum bdellium. Where possible, substitute similar substances—oils for oils, gums for gums, barks for barks, leaves for leaves and so on.

The third ingredient, gum armoniak, is today termed gum ammoniac. This is a gum resin obtained from both an Iranian tree as well as a species of *Ferula*. It is, again, impossible to find but you're still determined to create some form of Agrippa's Mars incense.

So you look up *Ferula* in *Cunningham's Encyclopedia of Magical Herbs* and discover that the common asafoetida is one species of *Ferula*. Asafoetida is also listed under the Mars table in this part. Success! But you know that asafoetida has an overpowering scent. Just a pinch should do.

Roots of both hellebors. "Hellebor" was a common spelling of hellebore during the 17th century. "Both" probably refers to *Helleborus niger*, black hellebore, as well as to white hellebore, a common folk name that was applied to several different plants.

Such a poisonous ingredient was probably included in this formula simply because it was poisonous. It is commercially unavailable today, and it would be an unwise magician who burned it in the censer. What else can you use? Look at the Mars listing. What about nettle? Sure, it isn't poisonous, but anyone who has touched a nettle knows that it stings. Such symbolism would make it a perfect candidate for an incense devoted to the "stinging" planet Mars. Nettle it is.

Loadstone. Maybe you have one of these natural magnets lying around the house. Lodestone (an alternate spelling) is traditionally attributed to Mars and/or Venus, so this inclusion fits. If you don't have a lodestone, just place a small artificial magnet into the finished product. Leave it there for a week or so and then remove before using. This will "magnetize" the incense with Martian powers.

Sulphur? No problem there. It's easily obtainable. If you don't have any, why not substitute a pinch of club moss (*Lycopodium clavatum*), or some other species of that common, primitive plant. Why is this plant used? One of its common names is "vegetable sulfur," due to its explosive nature. If you can't find club moss, decide that the asafoetida you've already included will do for the sulphur as well.

And finally, myrrh. If you have some, simply add it to the recipe. If not, substitute pine pitch or dragon's blood.

So, here's the original recipe with these suggested substitutions placed side-by-side:

| AGRIPPA'S MARS INCENSE | NEW MARS INCENSE |
| --- | --- |
| Euphorbium | Tobacco |
| Gum Bdellium | Copal/Pine resin/Dragon's Blood |
| Gum Armoniak | Asafoetida |
| Roots of both Hellebors | Nettle |
| Loadstone | Lodestone/Magnet |
| Sulphur | Sulphur/Club Moss/Asafoetida |
| Myrrh | Myrrh/Pine resin/Dragon's Blood |
| Brain of Cat/Blood of Bat | Omit *or* Egg White |

There! You've got a brand-new Mars incense built along the lines of a 16th-century recipe, which was either an adaptation or a recording of a much earlier formula. And you've successfully substituted every ingredient called for, no matter how strange or unavailable.

If you were to actually make this incense, it would be best to use several parts each of myrrh (or pine resin/dragon's blood) and copal, and a very slight amount of pipe tobacco, nettle and sulfur. The tiniest pinch of asafoetida—believe me—would be sufficient. A glob of egg white can also be added, but since you're probably not compounding a combustible incense, it can be omitted.

Whew! That's a good example of magical substitution. You probably won't need to work with such a difficult formula often, but if you do, you'll know the procedure.

Magical substitution isn't dangerous (remember the *Burning Sands of Araby?*) or against all magical tradition; nor will it render your herb compounds powerless so long as you follow these basic rules.

Don't fight substitution; work with it and enjoy it. It's a necessary and important aspect of magical herbalism.

# Tables of Magical Substitution

## Specific Substitutions

In order to increase the practicality of this book, I've devised this list of specific substitutions for several common and unusual herbs. It can be consulted when you lack an ingredient for an herbal mixture, as can the more general lists that follow.

Here are some additional guidelines:
• Rosemary can be safely used for any other herb.
• Rose for any flower.
• Frankincense or copal for any gum resin.
• Tobacco for any poisonous herb.

For other substitution ideas (particularly for oils), see Chapter 4.

Unless otherwise noted, all listings refer to plant materials, not oils.

ACACIA: Gum Arabic
ACACIA, GUM: Gum Arabic
ACONITE: Tobacco
ARABIC, GUM: Frankincense; Gum Mastic; Gum Tragacanth (for binding wet ingredients, not for incense use)
AMMONIAC, GUM: Asafoetida
ASAFOETIDA: Tobacco; Valerian
BALM OF GILEAD: Rose buds; Gum Mastic
BDELLIUM, GUM: Copal; Pine resin; Dragon's Blood
BELLADONNA: Tobacco
BENZOIN: Gum Arabic; Gum Mastic
CACHANA: Angelica root
CAMPHOR OIL: Eucalyptus oil; Lavender oil
CARNATION: Rose petals anointed with a few drops Clove oil

CASSIA: Cinnamon (Cinnamon sold in the U.S. is actually the less
    expensive cassia)
CASTOR BEAN: A few drops Castor oil
CEDAR: Sandalwood
CINQUEFOIL: Clover; Trefoil
CITRON: Equal parts Orange peel and Lemon peel
CLOVE: Mace; Nutmeg
CLOVER: Cinquefoil
COPAL: Frankincense; Cedar
COWBANE: Tobacco
CYPRESS: Juniper; Pine needles
DEERSTONGUE: Tonka bean (not for internal use); Woodruff;
    Vanilla
DITTANY OF CRETE: Gum Mastic
DRAGON'S BLOOD: Equal parts Frankincense and Red Sandalwood
EUCALYPTUS OIL: Camphor oil; Lavender oil
EUPHORBIUM: Tobacco
FRANKINCENSE: Copal; Pine resin
GALANGAL: Ginger root
GRAINS OF PARADISE: Black Pepper
GUM AMMONIAC: Asafoetida
GUM BDELLIUM: Copal; Pine resin; Dragon's Blood
HELLEBORE: Tobacco; Nettle
HEMLOCK: Tobacco
HEMP: Nutmeg; Damiana; Star Anise; Bay
HENBANE: Tobacco
HYSSOP: Lavender
IVY: Cinquefoil
JASMINE: Rose
JUNIPER: Pine
LAVENDER: Rose
LEMONGRASS: Lemon peel
LEMON PEEL: Lemongrass; Lemon peel
LEMON VERBENA: Lemongrass; Lemon peel
MACE: Nutmeg
MANDRAKE: Tobacco
MASTIC, GUM: Gum Arabic; Frankincense
MINT (any type): Sage
MISTLETOE: Mint; Sage
MUGWORT: Wormwood

NEROLI OIL: Orange oil
NIGHTSHADE: Tobacco
NUTMEG: Mace; Cinnamon
OAKMOSS: Patchouly
ORANGE: Tangerine peel
ORANGE FLOWERS: Orange peel
PATCHOULY: Oakmoss
PEPPERMINT: Spearmint
PEPPERWORT: Rue; Grains of Paradise; Black Pepper
PINE: Juniper
PINE RESIN: Frankincense; Copal
RED SANDALWOOD: Sandalwood mixed with a pinch of Dragon's
    Blood
ROSE: Yarrow
ROSE GERANIUM: Rose
RUE: Rosemary mixed with a pinch of Black Pepper
SAFFRON: Orange peel
SANDALWOOD: Cedar
SARSAPARILLA: Sassafras
SASSAFRAS: Sarsaparilla
SPEARMINT: Peppermint
SULFUR: Tobacco; Club Moss; Asafoetida
THYME: Rosemary
TOBACCO: Bay
TONKA BEAN: Deerstongue; Woodruff; Vanilla bean
TREFOIL: Cinquefoil
VALERIAN: Asafoetida
VANILLA: Woodruff; Deerstongue; Tonka Bean
VETIVERT: Calamus
WOLFSBANE: Tobacco
WOOD ALOE: Sandalwood sprinkled with Ambergris oil
WOODRUFF: Deerstongue; Vanilla
WORMWOOD: Mugwort
YARROW: Rose
YEW: Tobacco

### Key to the Tables

H = Herb, gum, flower, bark, root, leaf, fruit, seed
O = Essential oil, absolute
B = Bouquet
S = Synthetic

## Magical Goals

Not all magical goals are listed here. For those that are missing, see the following Planetary and Elemental tables, or check the Index. Use these lists for mixing your own blends or when substituting.

ASTRAL PROJECTION
Benzoin   H, O
Dittany of Crete   H
Cinnamon   H, O
Jasmine   H, O
Poplar   H
Sandalwood   H, O

COURAGE
Allspice   H
Black Pepper   H, O
Dragon's Blood   H
Frankincense   H, O
Geranium (Rose Geranium)   H, O
Sweet Pea   H, B
Tonka   H, B
Thyme   H

DIVINATION
Anise   H
Camphor   H, O
Clove   H, O
Hibiscus   H
Meadowsweet   H
Orange   H, O
Orris   H

EXORCISM
Angelica  H
Basil  H, O
Clove  H, O
Copal  H
Cumin  H
Dragon's Blood  H
Frankincense  H, O
Fumitory  H
Garlic  H
Heliotrope  H
Horehound  H
Juniper  H, O
Lilac  H
Mallow  H
Mistletoe  H
Myrrh  H, O
Pepper, Cayenne  H
Peppermint  H, O
Pine  H, O
Rosemary  H, O
Sagebrush  H
Sandalwood  H, O
Snapdragon  H
Thistle  H
Vetivert  H, O
Yarrow  H, O

HAPPINESS
Apple Blossom  H
Catnip  H
Hyacinth  H
Lavender  H, O
Marjoram  H
Meadowsweet  H
Sesame  H
Saffron  H
St. John's Wort  H

HEALING, HEALTH
Allspice  H
Angelica  H
Bay  H, O
Calamus  H
Carnation  H
Cedarwood  H, O
Cinnamon  H, O
Citron  H
Coriander  H, O
Eucalyptus  H, O
Fennel  H
Gardenia  H
Heliotrope  H
Honeysuckle  H
Juniper  H, O
Lemon Balm  H, O
Lime  H, O
Mugwort  H
Palmarosa  O
Pepper, Cayenne  H
Peppermint  H, O
Pine  H, O
Poppy seed  H
Rose  H, O
Rosemary  H, O
Saffron  H
Sandalwood  H, O
Sassafras  H
Spearmint  H, O
Spikenard  H
Thyme  H
Violet  H
Willow  H
Wintergreen  H
Yerba Santa  H

LOVE

| | |
|---|---|
| Apple Blossom  H, B | Marjoram  H |
| Apricot  O (no scent) | Mastic  H |
| Basil  H, O | Mimosa  H |
| Camomile  H, O | Myrtle  H |
| Catnip  H | Neroli  O |
| Chickweed  H | Orange  H, O |
| Cinnamon  H, O | Orchid  H |
| Civet  S | Orris  H |
| Clove  H, O | Palmarosa  O |
| Copal  H | Peppermint  H, O |
| Coriander  H, O | Plumeria  H |
| Cumin  H | Rose  H, O |
| Dill  H | Rosemary  H, O |
| Dragon's Blood  H | Sarsaparilla  H |
| Gardenia  H | Stephanotis  H |
| Geranium (Rose)  H, O | Sweet Pea  B |
| Ginger  H, O | Thyme  H |
| Hibiscus  H | Tonka  H, B |
| Jasmine  H, O | Tuberose  H, B |
| Juniper  H, O | Vanilla  H |
| Lavender  H, O | Vervain  H |
| Lemon  H, O | Vetivert  H, O |
| Lemon Balm  H, O | Violet  H |
| Lemon Verbena  H, O | Yarrow  H, O |
| Lime  H, O | Ylang-Ylang  O |
| Lotus  B | |

LUCK

| | |
|---|---|
| Allspice  H | Orange  H, O |
| Calamus  H | Poppy seed  H |
| Fern  H | Rose  H, O |
| Grains of Paradise  H | Spikenard  H |
| Hazel  H | Star Anise  H |
| Heather  H | Tonka  H, B |
| Irish Moss  H | Vetivert  H, O |
| Nutmeg  H, O | Violet  H |

LUST
Ambergris   S
Caraway   H
Cinnamon   H, O
Civet   S
Clove   H, O
Deerstongue   H
Ginger   H, O
Ginseng   H
Grains of Paradise   H
Hibiscus   H
Lemongrass   H, O
Nettle   H
Olive   H, O
Parsley   H
Patchouly   H, O
Peppermint   H, O
Rosemary   H, O
Saffron   H
Sesame   H
Stephanotis   H
Tuberose   H, B
Vanilla   H
Yerba Mate   H

MONEY AND RICHES
Allspice   H
Almond   H
Basil   H, O
Bergamot Mint   H, B
Calamus   H
Camomile   H, O
Cedarwood   H, O
Cinnamon   H, O
Cinquefoil   H
Clove   H, O
Clover   H
Dill   H
Elder   H
Galangal   H

Ginger   H, O
Heliotrope   H
Honeysuckle   H
Hyssop   H
Jasmine   H, O
Myrtle   H
Nutmeg   H, O
Oakmoss   H, B
Orange   H, O
Patchouly   H, O
Peppermint   H, O
Pine   H, O
Sage   H
Sassafras   H
Tonka   H, B
Vervain   H
Vetivert   H, O
Wood Aloe   H, O
Woodruff   H

PEACE
Cumin   H
Gardenia   H, B
Lavender   H, O
Lilac   H
Magnolia   B
Meadowsweet   H
Narcissus   H
Pennyroyal   H
Tuberose   H, B
Violet   H

POWER, MAGICAL
Allspice   H
Carnation   H
Dragon's Blood   H
Ginger   H, O
Gum Mastic   H
Tangerine   H, O
Vanilla   H

PROPHETIC (PSYCHIC) DREAMS

| | |
|---|---|
| Camphor  H, O | Marigold  H |
| Cinquefoil  H | Mimosa  H |
| Heliotrope  H | Rose  H, O |
| Jasmine  H, O | |

PROTECTION

| | |
|---|---|
| Angelica  H | Juniper  H, O |
| Anise  H, O | Lavender  H, O |
| Arabic, Gum  H | Lilac  H |
| Asafoetida  H | Lime  H, O |
| Balm of Gilead  H | Lotus  B |
| Basil  H, O | Mandrake  H |
| Bay  H, O | Marigold  H |
| Bergamot Mint  H, B | Mimosa  H |
| Black Pepper  H, O | Mistletoe  H |
| Calamus  H | Mugwort  H |
| Caraway  H | Myrrh  H, O |
| Carnation  H | Niaouli  O |
| Cedarwood  H, O | Orris  H |
| Cinnamon  H, O | Patchouly  H, O |
| Cinquefoil  H | Pennyroyal  H |
| Clove  H, O | Peony  H |
| Clover  H | Peppermint  H, O |
| Copal  H | Petitgrain  O |
| Cumin  H | Pine  H, O |
| Cypress  H, O | Rose  H, O |
| Dill  H | Rose Geranium  H, O |
| Dragon's Blood  H | Rue  H |
| Eucalyptus  H, O | Sage  H |
| Fennel  H | Sandalwood  H, O |
| Fern  H | Thistle  H |
| Flax  H | Valerian  H |
| Frankincense  H, O | Vervain  H |
| Galangal  H | Vetivert  H, O |
| Geranium (Rose)  H, O | Violet  H |
| Heather  H | Wood Aloe  H |
| Honeysuckle  H | Woodruff  H |
| Hyacinth  H | Wormwood  H |
| Hyssop  H | |

PSYCHIC AWARENESS
Acacia, Gum   H
Anise   H
Bay   H, O
Camphor   H, O
Cassia   H, O
Cinnamon   H, O
Citron   H
Clove   H, O
Flax   H
Galangal   H
Gardenia   H
Heliotrope   H
Honeysuckle   H
Lemongrass   H, O
Lilac   H
Mace   H, O
Marigold   H
Mastic, Gum   H
Mugwort   H
Nutmeg   H, O
Orange   H, O
Orris   H
Peppermint   H, O
Rose   H, O
Saffron   H
Star Anise   H
Thyme   H
Tuberose   H, B
Wormwood   H
Yarrow   H, O

PURIFICATION

| | |
|---|---|
| Anise  H | Lemon  H, O |
| Arabic, Gum  H | Lemon Verbena  H, O |
| Bay  H, O | Lime  H, O |
| Benzoin  H, O | Mimosa  H |
| Calamus  H | Musk  S |
| Camomile  H, O | Myrrh  H, O |
| Camphor  H, O | Parsley  H |
| Cedarwood  H, O | Peppermint  H, O |
| Cinnamon  H, O | Pine  H, O |
| Copal  H | Rosemary  H, O |
| Eucalyptus  H, O | Sandalwood  H, O |
| Fennel  H | Thyme  H |
| Frankincense  H, O | Tobacco  H |
| Hyssop  H | Valerian  H |
| Lavender  H, O | Vervain  H |

SPIRITUALITY

| | |
|---|---|
| Arabic, Gum  H | Lotus  B |
| Cassia  H, O | Myrrh  H, O |
| Cinnamon  H, O | Pine  H, O |
| Copal  H | Sage  H |
| Frankincense  H, O | Sandalwood  H, O |
| Gardenia  H | Wisteria  H |
| Heliotrope  H | Wood Aloe  H |
| Jasmine  H, O | |

## *Planetary Substitutions*

These lists are for use when compounding your own planetary blends or when substitution is necessary. Please note that all such correspondences are open to debate. I may change them from time to time as new information and insights into the nature of plants and the planets come to me. Broadly speaking, all are ritually appropriate. Some herbs appear in more than one section.

SUN

Recipes to promote healing, protection, success, illumination, magical power, physical energy, and to end legal matters.

| | |
|---|---|
| Acacia  H | Mastic, Gum  H |
| Arabic, Gum  H | Mistletoe  H |
| Bay  H, O | Oak  H |
| Benzoin  H, O | Orange  H, O |
| Carnation  H | Rosemary  H, O |
| Cedarwood  H, O | Sandalwood  H, O |
| Cinnamon  H, O | Tangerine  H, O |
| Citron  H | Wood Aloe  H |
| Copal  H | |
| Frankincense  H, O | |
| Juniper  H, O | |

MOON

Recipes to promote sleep, prophetic (psychic) dreams, psychic awareness, gardening, love, healing, fertility, peace, compassion, spirituality. Also for blends concerned with the family.

| | |
|---|---|
| Calamus  H | Lemon Balm  H, O |
| Camphor  H, O | Lotus  B |
| Coconut  H | Myrrh  H, O |
| Gardenia  H | Poppy seed  H |
| Grape  H | Sandalwood  H, O |
| Jasmine  H, O | Willow  H |
| Lemon  H, O | |

MERCURY

Recipes to promote intelligence, eloquence, divination, study, self-improvement; to help overcome addictions, break negative habits; for travel, communication, wisdom.

Almond   H
Bergamot Mint   H, B
Caraway   H
Dill   H
Fennel   H
Lavender   H, O
Lemongrass   H, O
Lemon Verbena   H, O
Peppermint   H, O
Thyme   H

VENUS

Recipes to promote love, fidelity, reconciliation, interchanges, beauty, youth, joy, happiness, pleasure, luck, friendship, compassion and meditation.

Apple Blossom   H
Cardamom   H, O
Crocus   H
Daisy   H
Geranium (Rose) H, O
Heather   H
Hyacinth   H
Iris   H
Licorice   H
Lilac   H
Magnolia   H, B
Myrtle   H
Orchid   H
Orris   H
Plumeria   H

Rose   H, O
Spearmint   H, O
Stephanotis   H
Sweet Pea   B
Tansy   H
Thyme   H
Tonka   H, B
Tuberose   H
'Vanilla   H
Violet   H
Willow   H
Ylang-Ylang   O

## MARS

Recipes to promote courage, aggression, healing after surgery, physical strength, politics, sexual energy, exorcism, protection and defensive magic.

Allspice   H
Asafoetida   H
Basil   H, O
Broom   H
Coriander   H, O
Cumin   H
Deerstongue   H
Dragon's Blood   H
Galangal   H
Ginger   H, O
Nettle   H
Peppermint   H, O
Pine   H, O
Tobacco   H
Woodruff   H
Wormwood   H

## JUPITER

Recipes to promote spirituality, meditation, money, prosperity, and to settle legal matters.

Anise   H
Cinquefoil   H
Clove   H, O
Honeysuckle   H
Hyssop   H
Maple   H
Nutmeg   H, O
Oakmoss   H, B
Sage   H
Sarsaparilla   H
Sassafras   H
Star Anise   H
Ti   H

SATURN

Recipes to promote protection, purification, longevity, exorcisms, vision, and endings, especially when concerned with the home.

Amaranth   H
Bistort   H
Comfrey   H
Cypress   H, O
Mimosa   H
Pansy   H
Patchouly   H, O
Tamarisk   H

## *Elemental Substitutions*

Before listing the herbs associated with each element, let's take a brief look at them.

The four elements (Earth, Air, Fire and Water) are the basic components of the universe. All that exists—or that has the potential to exist—is composed of one or more of these energies.

The most immediately recognizable manifestations of the elements are natural. A handful of dirt for Earth, a cloud moving in a breeze for Air, flame for Fire and a lake for Water. But the elements are much more than physical objects—*they are the energies behind all things,* manifest or unmanifest.

Many plants correspond to the elements. In turn, each element is associated with specific magical goals, as listed below. In burning an Air incense or anointing with a Fire oil we directly draw upon the element's energies to achieve her or his goal.

For the most potent effects, attune with the element before using one of its herbal products. Feel the heat of a fire when burning a Fire incense. Sense the purifying, moving energies of a stream when bathing in a Water bath. Imagine the rush of wind while anointing yourself with an Air oil. Smell the rich moistness of the Earth when using one of Her mixtures.

Elemental magic is one of the easiest forms to master, for it's all around us.*

Use these lists when compounding elemental mixtures, for creating your own recipes, or when substituting.

## EARTH

Recipes to promote peace, fertility, money, business success, stability, growth (as in gardens), employment and so on.

| | |
|---|---|
| Bistort  H | Oakmoss  H, B |
| Cypress  H, O | Patchouly  H, O |
| Fern  H | Primrose  H |
| Honeysuckle  H | Rhubarb  H |
| Horehound  H | Vervain  H |
| Magnolia  H, B | Vetivert  H, O |
| Mugwort  H | |
| Narcissus  H | |

## AIR

Recipes to promote communication, travel, intellect, eloquence, divination, freedom and wisdom.

| | |
|---|---|
| Acacia  H | Lemon Verbena  H, O |
| Arabic, Gum  H | Mace  H, O |
| Almond  H | Marjoram  H |
| Anise  H | Mastic, Gum  H |
| Benzoin  H, O | Parsley  H |
| Bergamot Mint  H, B | Peppermint  H, O |
| Citron  H | Sage  H |
| Lavender  H, O | Star Anise  H |
| Lemongrass  H, O | |

---

* See *Earth Power* for more Elemental magic.

FIRE

Recipes to promote communication, defensive magic, physical strength, magical power, courage, will power, purification.

Allspice   H
Angelica   H
Asafoetida   H
Basil   H, O
Bay   H, O
Carnation   H
Cedarwood   H, O
Cinnamon   H, O
Clove   H, O
Copal   H
Coriander   H, O
Deerstongue   H
Dill   H
Dragon's Blood   H
Fennel   H
Frankincense   H, O
Galangal   H, O
Garlic   H
Grains of Paradise   H
Heliotrope   H
Juniper   H, O
Lime   H, O
Marigold   H
Nutmeg   H, O
Orange   H, O
Peppermint   H, O
Rosemary   H, O
Rose Geranium   H, O
Sassafras   H
Tangerine   H, O
Tobacco   H
Woodruff   H

WATER

Recipes to promote love, healing, peace, compassion, reconciliation, purification, friendship, de-stressing, sleep, dreams and psychism.

| | |
|---|---|
| Apple Blossom  H | Lily  H |
| Balm, Lemon  H, O | Lotus  B |
| Calamus  H | Myrrh  H, O |
| Camomile  H, O | Orchid  H |
| Camphor  H, O | Orris  H |
| Cardamom  H, O | Passion Flower  H |
| Catnip  H | Peach  H |
| Cherry  H | Plumeria  H |
| Coconut  H | Rose  H, O |
| Comfrey  H | Sandalwood  H, O |
| Elder  H | Spearmint  H, O |
| Eucalyptus  H, O | Stephanotis  H |
| Gardenia  H | Sweet Pea  B |
| Heather  H | Tansy  H |
| Hyacinth  H | Thyme  H |
| Iris  H | Tonka  H, B |
| Jasmine  H, O | Vanilla  H |
| Lemon  H, O | Violet  H |
| Licorice  H | Ylang-Ylang  O |
| Lilac  H | |

## *Astrological Substitutions*

Use these lists for creating your own blends or for substituting. If none of these herbs are available when you need to substitute, look to the sign's ruling planet for further suggestions.

### ARIES (ruled by Mars)

| | |
|---|---|
| Allspice H | Dragon's Blood H |
| Carnation H | Fennel H |
| Cedarwood H, O | Frankincense H, O |
| Cinnamon H, O | Galangal H |
| Clove H, O | Juniper H, O |
| Copal H | Musk S |
| Cumin H | Peppermint H, O |
| Deerstongue H | Pine H, O |

### TAURUS (ruled by Venus)

| | |
|---|---|
| Apple Blossom H | Patchouly H, O |
| Cardamom H, O | Plumeria H |
| Daisy H | Rose H, O |
| Honeysuckle H | Thyme H |
| Lilac H | Tonka H, B |
| Magnolia H, B | Vanilla H |
| Oakmoss H, B | Violet H |
| Orchid H | |

### GEMINI (Ruled by Mercury)

| | |
|---|---|
| Almond H | Lavender H, O |
| Anise H | Lemongrass H, O |
| Bergamot Mint H, B | Lily H |
| Citron H | Mace H, O |
| Clover H | Mastic, Gum H |
| Dill H | Parsley H |
| Horehound H | Peppermint H, O |

## CANCER (MOONCHILDREN; ruled by the Moon)

| | |
|---|---|
| Ambergris  S | Lilac  H |
| Calamus  H | Lotus  B |
| Eucalyptus  H, O | Myrrh  H, O |
| Gardenia  H, B | Rose  H, O |
| Jasmine  H, O | Sandalwood  H, O |
| Lemon  H, O | Violet  H |
| Lemon Balm  H, O | |

## LEO (ruled by the Sun)

| | |
|---|---|
| Acacia  H | Juniper  H, O |
| Benzoin  H, O | Musk  S |
| Cinnamon  H, O | Nutmeg  H, O |
| Copal  H | Orange  H, O |
| Frankincense  H, O | Rosemary  H, O |
| Heliotrope  H | Sandalwood  H, O |

## VIRGO (ruled by Mercury)

| | |
|---|---|
| Almond  H | Lavender  H, O |
| Bergamot Mint  H, B | Lily  H, O |
| Cypress  H, O | Mace  H, O |
| Dill  H | Moss  H |
| Fennel  H | Patchouly  H, O |
| Honeysuckle  H | Peppermint  H, O |

## LIBRA (ruled by Venus)

| | |
|---|---|
| Apple Blossom  H | Plumeria  H |
| Catnip  H | Rose  H, O |
| Lilac  H | Spearmint  H, O |
| Magnolia  H, B | Sweet Pea  B |
| Marjoram  H | Thyme  H |
| Mugwort  H | Vanilla  H |
| Orchid  H | Violet  H |

## SCORPIO (ruled by Mars, Pluto)

| | |
|---|---|
| Allspice  H | Gardenia  H |
| Ambergris  S | Ginger  H, O |
| Basil  H, O | Myrrh  H, O |
| Clove  H, O | Pine  H, O |
| Cumin  H | Vanilla  H |
| Deerstongue  H | Violet  H |
| Galangal  H | |

## SAGITTARIUS (ruled by Jupiter)

| | |
|---|---|
| Anise  H | Honeysuckle  H |
| Carnation  H | Juniper  H, O |
| Cedarwood  H, O | Nutmeg  H, O |
| Clove  H, O | Orange  H, O |
| Copal  H | Rose  H, O |
| Deerstongue  H | Sage  H |
| Dragon's Blood  H | Sassafras  H |
| Frankincense  H, O | Star Anise  H |
| Ginger  H, O | |

## CAPRICORN (ruled by Saturn)

| | |
|---|---|
| Cypress  H, O | Oakmoss  H, B |
| Honeysuckle  H | Patchouly  H, O |
| Magnolia  H, B | Vervain  H |
| Mimosa  H | Vetivert  H, O |

## AQUARIUS (ruled by Saturn and Uranus)

| | |
|---|---|
| Acacia  H | Mace  H, O |
| Almond  H | Mastic, Gum  H |
| Benzoin  H, O | Mimosa  H |
| Citron  H | Patchouly  H, O |
| Cypress  H, O | Peppermint  H, O |
| Lavender  H, O | Pine  H, O |

PISCES (ruled by Jupiter and Neptune)

| | |
|---|---|
| Anise  H | Mimosa  H |
| Calamus  H | Nutmeg  H, O |
| Catnip  H | Orris  H |
| Clove  H, O | Sage  H |
| Eucalyptus  H, O | Sandalwood  H, O |
| Gardenia  H | Sarsaparilla  H, O |
| Honeysuckle  H, O | Star Anise  H |
| Jasmine  H, O | Sweet Pea  B |
| Lemon  H, O | |

# Glossary

MANY OF THESE definitions are exclusive to magic, magical herbalism and perfumery. Naturally, these definitions are my own, based on deduction and personal experience. **Luck, Good** is a prime example.

Italicized terms refer to other related entries in the Glossary.

**Akasha:** The fifth element, the omnipresent spiritual power that permeates the universe. It is the energy out of which the *Elements* formed.

**Amulet:** A magically *empowered* object that deflects specific, usually negative, energies. Generally, a protective object. (Compare with *Talisman*.)

**Anaphrodisiac:** A substance, such as camphor, that reduces sexual desires.

**Aphrodisiac:** A substance that produces sexual excitement.

**Asperger:** A bundle of fresh herbs or a perforated object used for purificatory purposes to sprinkle water during or preceding ritual.

**Astral Projection:** The act of separating the consciousness from the physical body and moving it about at will.

**Bane, Baneful:** That which destroys life. Poisonous, dangerous, destructive. Herbs such as henbane, hellebore and aconite are examples of baneful substances.

**Banish:** The magical act of driving away evil or negativity. A strong purification, sometimes associated with the removal of "spirits."

**Beltane:** A *Wiccan* festival celebrated on April 30th or May 1st. Beltane celebrates the symbolic union of the Goddess and God (the

Wiccan deities). It links in with the approaching Summer months.

**Bouquet:** In perfumery, a blend of natural or synthetic scents which reproduces a specific odor, such as rose or jasmine. Also known as a compound or a blend.

**Brew:** *See Infusion.*

**Censer:** A heat-proof container in which incense is smoldered; an incense burner or any similar object.

**Circle, Magic:** *See Magic Circle.*

**Combustible Incense:** Self-burning incense containing potassium nitrate; usually in cone, block or stick form.

**Conscious Mind:** The societally controlled, intellectual, theorizing, materialistic half of the human mind that is at work in everyday activities. Compare with *Psychic Mind.*

**Consecration:** A *ritual* of sanctification or purification. A ritual of dedication.

**Curse:** A conscious direction of negative energy toward a person, place or thing.

**Divination:** The magical act of discovering the unknown by interpreting random patterns or symbols through the use of tools such as clouds, tarot cards, flames, smoke. Divination contacts the *psychic mind* by tricking, or "drowsing," the *conscious mind* through *ritual* and observation of, or manipulation of, tools. Divination isn't necessary for those who can easily attain communication with the *psychic mind*, though they may practice it.

**Elements, The:** Earth, Air, Fire and Water. These four essences are the building blocks of the universe. Everything that exists (or that has potential to exist) contains one or more of these energies. The elements hum within ourselves and are also at large in the world. They can be utilized to cause change through *magic*. The four elements formed from the primal essence, or power—*Akasha.*

**Empower, Empowering:** The movement of personal energies into herbs, stones or other objects. The empowered objects are then used in *magic*. In *herb magic*, empowering aligns the energies within herbs with magical goals.

**Enfleurage:** A French perfumery term describing the process of extracting essential flower oils with purified fat. Also known as *pommade.*

**Esbat:** A Wiccan ritual occasion celebrating the Full Moon. Compare with *Sabbat. See also Wicca.*

**Evocation:** Calling up spirits or other nonphysical entities, either to visible appearance or invisible attendance. Compare with *Invocation*.

**Exorcism:** Traditionally, the magical process of driving out negative entities. In *herb magic*, a powerful purification.

**Grimoire:** A magical workbook with information on *rituals*, magical properties of natural objects, preparation of ritual equipment. Many include "catalogues of spirits." The most famous of the old grimoires is probably *The Key of Solomon* (see Bibliography under Mathers). Most were first committed to paper in the 16th and 17th centuries, though they may be far older.

**Handfasting:** A *Wiccan, Pagan* or Gypsy wedding. More broadly, any wedding or solemn betrothal.

**Herb:** A plant used in magic. Herbs are usually strongly scented and are prized for their specific energies. Includes trees, ferns, grasses, seaweeds, vegetables, fruits and flowering plants.

**Herbalism:** The practice of cultivating, gathering and using plants for medicinal, cosmetic, ritual and culinary purposes. *See Herb Magic.*

**Herb Magic:** The practice of directing energies found within plants to create needed change. A branch of *magic*. Practitioners utilize *personal power* as well as other forms of energy, such as colors, candles, stones, sounds, gestures and movements.

**Hex:** *See Curse.*

**Imbolc:** A *Wiccan* festival celebrated on February 2nd. Imbolc marks the first stirrings of Spring and is a traditional time to practice magic.

**Incubus:** A male demon or spirit that was believed to sexually tempt and abuse women. Compare with *Succubus*.

**Infusion:** A liquid produced by soaking herbs in very hot (but not boiling) water. A brew or potion.

**Invocation:** An appeal or petition to a specific conception of Deity. A prayer. A request for a deity's appearance or attendance during a *ritual*. Also, a mystical practice that produces an awareness of Deity within. Compare with *Evocation*.

**Luck, Good:** An individual's ability to make timely, correct decisions, to perform correct actions and to place herself or himself in positive situations. "Bad luck" stems from ignorance and an unwillingness to accept self-responsibility.

**Lughnasadh:** A *Wiccan* festival celebrated on August 1st. Lughnasadh marks the first harvest and the symbolic ebbing of the Sun's energies.

**Mabon:** A *Wiccan* festival celebrated on or around September 21st, the Autumnal Equinox, which marks the second harvest. Autumn transmutes into Winter. A time of thanks and reflection.

**Magic:** The movement of natural energies (such as *personal power*) to create needed change. Energy exists within all things: ourselves, plants, stones, colors, sounds, movements. Magic is the process of "rousing" or building up this energy, giving it purpose, then releasing it. Magic is a natural, not supernatural, practice, though it is little understood. *See Herb Magic.*

**Magic Circle:** A sphere constructed of *personal power* in which *Wiccan* or magical rituals are often enacted. The term refers to the circle that marks the sphere's penetration of the ground, for it extends above and below the ground. It is created through *visualization* and *magic.*

**Meditation:** Reflection, contemplation, turning inward toward the self or outward toward Deity or nature. A quiet time in which the practitioner may dwell upon particular thoughts or symbols, or allow them to come unbidden.

**Midsummer:** The Summer Solstice (on or around June 21st), one of the *Wiccan* festivals and an excellent night for magic. Midsummer marks the point of the year when the Sun is symbolically at the height of its powers.

**Noncombustible Incense:** Incense which is compounded without potassium nitrate, and which requires heat to release its scent. Compare with *Combustible Incense.*

**Ostara:** A *Wiccan* festival occurring at the Spring Equinox (on or around March 21st), which marks the beginning of true Spring. A Fire festival celebrating the resurgence of Earth fertility, and an ideal time for magic.

**Pagan:** From the Latin *paganus,* meaning country dweller. Today, used as a general term for followers of *Wicca* and other shamanistic, polytheistic and magic-embracing religions.

**Pentagram:** The basic five-pointed star, visualized with one point upward. The pentagram represents the five senses, the *Elements* (Earth, Air, Fire, Water and *Akasha*), the hand and the human body. It is a protective symbol known to have been in use since the days of old Babylon. Today it is frequently associated with *Wicca.* A symbol of power.

**Personal Power:** The energy which sustains our bodies, and which is available for use in *magic.*

**Psychic Mind:** The subconscious, or unconscious, mind in which we receive psychic impulses. The psychic mind is at work when we sleep, dream and meditate. *Divination* is a ritual process designed to contact the psychic mind. *Intuition* is a term used to describe psychic information that unexpectedly reaches the conscious mind. *Psychism* describes the state in which information from the psychic mind is available to the conscious mind.

**Psychism:** The act of being consciously psychic. *Ritual consciousness* is a form of psychism.

**Reincarnation:** The doctrine of rebirth. The process of repeated incarnations in human form to allow evolution of the sexless, ageless soul.

**Ritual:** Ceremony. A specific form of movement, manipulation of objects or inner processes designed to produce desired effects. In religion, ritual is geared toward union with the divine. In *magic* it produces a specific state of consciousness that allows the magician to move energy toward needed goals. A *spell* is a magical ritual.

**Ritual Consciousness:** A specific, alternate state of awareness necessary to the successful practice of magic. The magician achieves this through the use of *visualization* and *ritual*. It denotes a state in which the *conscious mind* and *psychic mind* are attuned, wherein the magician senses energies, gives them purpose and releases them towards the magical goal. It is a heightening of the senses, an expansion of the awareness beyond the physical world, an interlinking with nature and with the forces behind all conceptions of Deity.

**Sabbat:** A *Wiccan* festival. *See Beltane, Imbolc, Lughnasadh, Mabon, Midsummer, Ostara, Samhain* and *Yule.*

**Sachet:** A cloth bag filled with herbs. In *herb magic* sachets are used to contain herb mixtures while they slowly release their energies for specific magical goals.

**Samhain:** A *Wiccan* festival celebrated on October 31st. Samhain is a gathering up of energies before the depths of Winter. An ancient night upon which to perform magic.

**Scry, To:** To gaze at or into an object (a quartz crystal sphere, pool of water, reflections, a candle flame) to still the *conscious mind* and to contact the *psychic mind*. This allows the scryer to become aware of possible events prior to their actual occurrence, as well as to perceive past or present events through other than the five senses. A form of *divination*.

**Spell:** A magical *ritual*, usually nonreligious in nature and often accompanied by spoken works.

**Succubus:** A female spirit or demon once believed to sexually tempt and abuse men. It may have been a theological explanation of nocturnal emissions. Compare with *Incubus.*

**Talisman:** An object *empowered* with magical energy to attract a specific force or energy to its bearer. Compare with *Amulet.*

**Tincture:** A liquid produced by soaking plant materials in ethyl alcohol (or medicinally, in apple cider vinegar) to produce a scented liquid.

**Visualization:** The process of forming mental images. Magical visualization consists of forming images of needed goals during *ritual*. Visualization is also used to direct *personal power* and natural energies during *magic* for various purposes, including *empowering* and forming the *magic circle*. It is a function of the *conscious mind.*

**Wicca:** A contemporary *pagan* religion with spiritual roots in the earliest expressions of reverence for nature. Wicca views Deity as Goddess and God; thus, it is polytheistic. It also embraces *magic* and *reincarnation*. Some Wiccans identify themselves with the word *Witch.*

**Wiccan:** A follower of *Wicca.* Alternately, denoting some aspect of that religion.

**Witch:** Anciently, a European practitioner of the remnants of pre-Christian folk magic, especially *herb magic* and *herbalism*. One who practiced *Witchcraft*. Later this term's meaning was deliberately altered to denote demented, dangerous, supernatural beings who practiced destructive magic and who threatened Christianity. This was a political, monetary and sexist move on the part of organized religion. The latter meaning is still currently accepted by many non-Witches. The term *Witch* is sometimes used by members of *Wicca* to describe themselves.

**Witchcraft:** The *craft* of the *Witch*—*magic*, especially magic utilizing *personal power* in conjunction with the energies within stones, *herbs,* colors and other natural objects. Some followers of *Wicca* use this word to denote their religion, producing much confusion on the part of outsiders.

**Wort:** An old term meaning *herb*. Mugwort preserves the word.

**Yule:** A *Wiccan* festival celebrated on or about December 21st, marking the rebirth of the Sun God from the Goddess. A time of joy and celebration during the miseries of Winter. Yule occurs on the Winter Solstice.

# *Appendix 1: Colors*

THIS TABLE OF colors and their energies can be used when choosing candles for spells, for tinting bath salts, and for designing entire rituals around your herbal products. Though these ritual associations are generally accepted, some differences in thought do exist. Color is a magical system in and of itself.*

**WHITE:** Protection, purification, peace, truth, sincerity

**RED:** Protection, strength, health, vigor, lust, sex, passion, courage, exorcism

**BLACK:** Absorbing and destroying negativity, healing severe diseases, banishing

**LIGHT BLUE:** Tranquility, healing, patience, happiness

**DARK BLUE:** Change, flexibility, the subconscious mind, psychism, healing

**GREEN:** Finances, money, fertility, prosperity, growth, luck, employment

**GRAY:** Neutrality

**YELLOW:** Intellect, attraction, study, persuasion, confidence, divination

**BROWN:** Working magic for animals, healing animals, the home

**PINK:** Love, honor, morality, friendships

**ORANGE:** Adaptability, stimulation, attraction

**PURPLE:** Power, healing severe diseases, spirituality, meditation

---

* See Raymond Buckland's *Practical Color Magick* (Llewellyn, 1984).

# *Appendix 2: Sources*

One of the regrettable omissions in the first edition of this book was a listing of reputable mail-order suppliers of herbs, essential oils, live herb plants and other materials. With my apologies, here it is.

APHRODISIA
264 Bleeker St.
New York, NY 10014
(212) 989-6440
Fax (212) 989-8027
A wide selection of dried herbs.

AROMA VERA INC.
5901 Rodeo Rd.
Los Angeles, CA 90016
(310) 280-0407
web site: aromavera.com
True essential oils.

COMPANION PLANTS
7247 N. Coolville Ridge Rd.
Athens, OH 45701
(740) 592-4643
Hundreds of rare and unusual herbs and plants. Live or seeds.

THE CRYSTAL CAVE
415 W. Foothill Blvd.
Claremont, CA 91711
(909) 626-0398
e-mail: cryscavldy@aol.com
web site: www.merlinscrystalcave.com
Dried herbs, charcoal blocks, candles, censers and crystals, books. Ask about availability of copal.

ENCHANTMENTS
341 E. 9th St.
New York, NY 10003
(212) 228-4394
Herbs, candles, charcoal blocks.

EYE OF THE CAT
3314 E. Broadway
Long Beach, CA 90803
(562) 438-3569
A huge stock of common and unusual dried herbs, charcoal blocks,
candles, books.

FIREWIND HERBAL PRODUCTS
P.O. Box 5527
Hopkins, MN 55343
(612) 543-9065
Firewindhp.com
Herbs, resins, charcoal, censers and more.

ISIS
5701 E. Colfax Ave.
Denver, CO 80220
(303) 321-0867
web site: www.ISISBOOKS.com
Dried herbs and oils, candles, charcoal blocks and books.

MAGICK BOOKSTORE
2306 Highland Ave.
National City, CA 91950
(619) 477-5260
e-mail: MAGICKBOOK@aol.com
Dried herbs, candles, books. Free catalog.

ORIGINAL SWISS AROMATICS
P.O. Box 606
San Rafael, CA 94915
(415) 479-3979
True essential oils.

# Bibliography

THIS BOOK IS the product of personal experimentation, much of which was based on suggestions by friends and teachers. However, there are published sources that are of value to the student who wishes to further research the subject of magical perfumery.

Some of these works contain only a fragment of magically oriented information. Others are magical textbooks. Distinction between these two extremes is made in the notes.

Additionally, many of these books print recipes not included in this work. I don't agree with all or even anything that the below authors have to say, but that doesn't mean that their books shouldn't be consulted.

The literature of magical herb products is even more limited than that of herb magic in general; hence, many of these works concentrate on the *processes* of herb magic—creating perfumes, soaps, incenses, ointments and so on—rather than on the magic itself.

Unfortunately, most of the classic books on this subject are out of print; but they can still be found in secondhand book stores, some libraries, or by mail from book-search services.

Utilize the information you find in them along magical lines. The processes described can easily be transferred to magical ends by choosing ingredients in harmony with your goal and by empowering the products once they're made.

Agrippa, Henry Cornelius. *The Philosophy of Natural Magic.* Antwerp, 1531. Reprint. Chicago: de Laurence, 1919. Reprint. Secaucus NJ: University Books, 1974.
This work contains the first volume of Agrippa's Three Books of

Occult Philosophy. Later additions, which are rather quaint, are also included. As I mentioned in Part III, some of the translations seem questionable. See the next entry.

Agrippa, Henry Cornelius. *Three Books of Occult Philosophy.* 1533. English translation first published in London, 1651. Reprint. London: Chthonios Books, 1986.

This is the first publication of Agrippa's complete magical work in over 300 years. These books gathered together much of the magical lore of his time—particularly that concerning plants, animals, stones, the planets and the elements. Of special interest are his "fume" recipes and his planetary attributions of plants. A classic work.

Aima. *Ritual Book of Herbal Spells.* Los Angeles: Foibles, 1976. A book of herb magic culled from a wide variety of sources, this good book includes many formulas for incenses (some of which are quite complex in the range of ingredients). A worthwhile book.

Arctander, Steffen. *Perfume and Flavor Materials of Natural Origin.* Elizabeth, NJ: Published by the author, 1960.

A scholarly look at essential oils—their manufacture, properties and the materials used. No magical information.

Bailes, Edith G. *An Album of Fragrance.* Richmond, Maine: Cardamom Press, 1983.

A delightful booklet of herbal recipes and processing techniques for creating incenses, oils and sachets. The author includes detailed instructions for *enfleurage* using purified fat, but includes no ritual information.

Barrett, Francis. *The Magus: A Complete System of Occult Philosophy.* Secaucus, NJ: University Books, 1967.

This book contains most of the standard incense formulas used in ceremonial magic of earlier centuries. Barrett compiled these in the late 1700s and was heavily influenced by Agrippa. *The Magus* is now available in an oversize paperback edition.

Conway, David. *Magic: An Occult Primer.* New York: Bantam, 1972.

Mr. Conway includes many interesting formulas for flying ointments and similar dangerous substances, but he fails to warn the reader of the attendant hazards of using them. Interesting, but I wouldn't recommend trying them.

Conway, David. *The Magic of Herbs.* New York: Dutton, 1973.

This book includes a few ancient formulas and a section on herbal narcotics, as well as a look at herbalism and astrology.

Devine, M. V. *Brujeria: A Study in Mexican-American Folk-Magic.* St. Paul: Llewellyn Publications, 1982.

Ms. Devine includes several incense and oil recipes here, some of which I've reproduced in this book with her permission. A wonderful, witty work.

Duff, Gail. *A Book of Potpourri: New and Old Ideas for Fragrant Flowers and Herbs.* New York: Beaufort Books, 1985.

This beautifully illustrated book contains a wealth of formulas and ideas for incense, scented inks, soaps and many other herbal products, though the focus here is on cosmetic rather than ritual magic.

Fettner, Ann Tucker. *Potpourri, Incense and Other Fragrant Concoctions.* New York: Workman, 1977.

This delightful book contains a section on incense, including directions for fashioning cone incense. Complete recipes are given for creating non-occult mixtures.

Griffith, F. L. and Herbert Thompson, eds. *The Leyden Papyrus: An Egyptian Magical Book.* New York: Dover, 1974.

This third-century Egyptian magical papyrus contains some curious herbal magic, much of which is barely comprehensible.

Hansen, Harold A. *The Witch's Garden.* Santa Cruz, CA: Unity Press, 1978.

A look at the flying ointments of days past. Not a practical book, though I've seen it touted as such. The emphasis is on the heavily negative aspects of herbalism (poisons, drugs). A depressing, biased book. Not recommended unless you're interested in such things.

Hayes, Carolyn H. *Pergemin: Perfumes, Incenses, Colors, Birthstones: Their Occult Properties and Uses.* Chicago: Aries Press, 1937.

This wonderful little booklet, now unfortunately long out of print, contains an excellent incense section as well as much interesting information about oils, with many recipes.

Huson, Paul. *Mastering Herbalism.* New York: Stein and Day, 1974.

This book contains a good chapter on perfumes (oils) and incense composition, offering several interesting recipes.

Junius, Manfred M. *Practical Handbook of Plant Alchemy.* New York: Inner Traditions International, 1985.

An advanced treatise regarding the "lesser work" of laboratory alchemy.

Leyel, C. F. *The Magic of Herbs.* New York: Harcourt, Brace and Company, 1926. Reprint. Toronto: Coles, 1981.

Truly a classic work, *The Magic of Herbs* contains a wonderful chapter on perfumes and perfumers, including many, many recipes from ancient sources. A must book for the serious magical herbalist!

Malbrough, Ray. *Charms, Spells and Formulas.* St. Paul: Llewellyn Publications, 1986.

An authentic guide to Louisiana Hoodoo magic, containing many great incense, oil, powder and wash recipes. Real Cajun magic.

Maple, Eric. *The Magic of Perfume.* New York: Weiser, 1973. This short introduction to the world of magical scents is curiously comprehensive—and well worthwhile.

Mathers, S. Liddell MacGregor, ed. and trans. *The Key of Solomon the King (Clavicula Salomonis).* 1888. Reprint. New York: Samuel Weiser, 1972.

This work, a translation of perhaps the most famous of all grimoires, contains some ink exorcisms, an asperger formula and a bit of other herbal information.

Meyer, David. *Sachets, Potpourri and Incense Recipes.* Glenwood, IL: Meyerbooks, 1986.

This booklet is a compilation of recipes and processes. It includes a short section describing materials used in herbal perfumery. No magical information.

Moldenke, Harold N. and Alma L. *Plants of the Bible.* Waltham, MA: Chronica Botanica Company, 1952.

A scholarly look at the herbs, barks and resins used in religion and magic in the Near East nearly 2,000 years ago.

Paulsen, Kathryn. *Witches' Potions and Spells.* Mount Vernon, NY: Peter Pauper Press, 1971.

A charming compendium of spells culled from ancient sources, this book contains many brew recipes, although some of them include the usual nasty substances.

Poucher, William A. *Perfumes, Cosmetics and Soaps.* 3 Vols. Princeton, NJ: D. Van Nostrad and Co., Inc., 1958.

An intelligent, in-depth look at the ingredients in, and the blending of, perfumes and cosmetics. Unfortunately, this work lacks magical information.

Salat, Barbara and David Copperfield, eds. *Well-Being: Advice from* the *Do-It-Yourself Journal for Healthy Living*. Garden City, NY: Anchor Press/Doubleday, 1979.

An excellent introduction to herbalism, containing much information on creating your own herbal remedies, cosmetics, and so on, with soap recipes. No magical lore is included.

Slater, Herman ed. *The Magical Formulary*. New York: Magickal Childe, 1981.

This work concentrates on Voodoo-type formulas for incenses, oils and powders, with a healthy sampling of Wiccan and ceremonial magic formulas as well. Pass over the hexing recipes, which were unfortunately included.

Tarotstar. *The Witch's Formulary and Spellbook*. New York: Original Publications, n.d.

An assortment of recipes for incenses, oils, inks and so on, much of it "black-arts" (i.e., negative, cursing, hexing) formulas. A good basic sourcebook if you can overlook the negative information.

Thompson, C. J. S. *The Mysteries and Secrets of Magic*. New York: The Olympia Press, 1972.

This fascinating work includes a chapter concerned with incenses, as well as much magical information otherwise unavailable.

Thompson, C. J. S. *The Mystery and Lure of Perfume*. Philadelphia: J. B. Lippincott, 1927.

A fabulous book devoted to perfumes, incenses and other scented goods of ancient times. Several recipes are given.

Traven, Beatrice. *The Complete Book of Natural Cosmetics*. New York: Simon and Schuster, 1974.

A chapter on creating natural perfumes is included in this work, but again, no magical information is given.

Verrill, A. Hyatt. *Perfumes and Spices*. New York: L. C. Page and Co., 1940.

A detailed account of perfumery, with many interesting tips on blending oils and recipes as well (though non-magical in nature). Much of this information seems to have come from Poucher (see above).

Vinci, Leo. *Incense: Its Ritual Significance, Use and Preparation*. New York: Weiser, 1980.

A useful little book with many recipes and hints, as well as directions for making cone incense.

# Botanical Index

COMMON NAMES ARE just that—common. They vary from country to country and even from district to district. The variety of common names is confusing. Therefore, I've included the following list of plants mentioned in this book together with their Latin names to facilitate identification.

Exact identification for some plants is difficult due to a number of factors. In these cases only the genus is given.

Acacia, Gum—*Acacia senegal*
x Aconite—*Aconitum napellus*
~ Acorn (fruit of the oak)—*Quercus alba*
Agrimony—*Agrimonia eupatoria*
Allspice—*Pimenta officinalis* or *P. dioica*
Almond—*Prunus dulcis*
Aloe, Wood—*Aquilaria agallocha*
Amaranth—*Amaranthus hypochondriacus*
Ambrette—*Hibiscus abelmoschus*
~ P Angelica—*Angelica archangelica*
Anise—*Pimpinella anisum*
Apple—*Pyrus* spp.
Apricot—*Prunus armeniaca*
Arabic, Gum—*Acacia vera*
Asafoetida—*Ferula asafoetida*
Ash—*Fraxinus excelsior; F. americana*
Avens—*Geum urbanum*

255

    Baby's Breath—*Gypsophila paniculata*
*x*  Balm of Gilead—*Commiphora opobalsamum*
    Barley—*Hordeum* spp.
*P*  Basil—*Ocimum basilicum*
    Bay—*Laurus nobilis*
    Bayberry—*Myrica* spp.
    Bdellium, Gum—*Bursera* spp.
    Beet—*Beta vulgaris*
*x*  Belladonna—*Atropa belladonna*
    Benzoin—*Styrax benzoin*
*P*  Bergamot—*Mentha citrata*
    Betony, Wood—*Betonica officinalis*
    Birch—*Betula alba*
    Birthwort—*Aristolochia clematitis*
    Bistort—*Polygonum bistorta*
    Blackberry—*Rubus villosus*
*x*  Black Hellebore—*Helleborus niger*
*x*  Black Nightshade—*Solanum nigrum*
    Black Pepper—*Piper nigrum*
    Black Tea—*Thea sinensis*
~*P*  Bladderwrack—*Fucus visiculosis*
    Broom—*Cytisus scoparius*
*x*  Bryony—*Bryony* spp.
*P*  Buchu—*Agathosma betulina or Baromsa betulina*

    Cachana—*Liatris punctata*
    Calamint—*Calamintha* spp.
*x*  Calamus—*Acorus calamus*
*P*  Camomile—*Anthemis nobilis*  German Camomile okay for *P*
*x*  Camphor—*Cinnamomum camphora*
    Caper—*Capparis spinosa*
    Caraway—*Carum carvi*
    Cardamom—*Elettario cardamomum*
*x*  Carnation—*Dianthus carophyllus*
    Cassia—*Cinnamomum cassia*
    Castor—*Ricinus communis*
*P*  Catnip—*Nepeta cataria*
    Cayenne—*Capsicum frutescens*
    Cedar—*Cedrus libani* or *Cedrus* spp.
    Chicory—*Chicorium intybus*

Chrysanthemum—*Chrysanthemum* spp.
Cinnamon—*Cinnamomum zeylanicum*
Cinquefoil—*Potentilla canadensis* or *P. reptans*
Citron—*Citrus medica*
Clove—*Syzygium aromaticum* or *Carophyllus aromaticus*
~ P Clover—*Trifolium* spp.
Club Moss—*Lycopodium clavatum*
Coconut—*Cocos nucifera*
x Comfrey—*Symphytum officinale*
Copal—*Bursera* spp.
Coriander—*Coriandrum sativum*
Corn—*Zea mays*
Costmary—*Balsamita major*
Costus—*Aplotaxis lappa*
Crocus—*Crocus vernus*
Cubeb—*Piper cubeb*
Cucumber—*Cucumis sativus*
Cumin—*Cumimum cyminum*
P Cypress—*Cupressus sempervirens*

Damiana—*Turnera diffusa* or *T. aphrodisiaca*
x Deadly Nightshade—*Solanum* spp.
x Deerstongue—*Frasera speciosa* or *Liatris odoratissimus*
Dill—*Anethum graveolens*
Dittany of Crete—*Dictamus origanoides*
Dock—*Rumex* spp.
Dogwood—*Cornus florida*
Dragon's Blood—*Daemonorops draco* or *Draceaena* spp.

Elder—*Sambucus canadensis*
x Eucalyptus—*Eucalyptus* spp.
x Euphorbium—*Euphorbia* spp.
Eyebright—*Euphrasia officinalis*

Fennel—*Foeniculum vulgare*
x Fern—various plants
~ Flax—*Linum usitatissimum*
Fleawort—*Inula conyza*
Frankincense—*Boswellia carterii*
Fumitory—*Fumaria officinalis*

Galangal—*Alpina officinalis* or *A. galanga*
Gall nuts (Oak galls from *Quercus alba?*)
Gardenia—*Gardenia* spp.
Garlic—*Allium sativum*
*x* Geranium (scented varieties)—*Pelargonium* spp.
Ginger—*Zingiber officinalis*
Grains of Paradise—*Aframomum melequeta*
Grape—*Vitis vinifera*
Grapefruit—*Citrus paradisi*
Ground Ivy—*Nepeta hederacea*
Gum Acacia—*Acacia senegal*
Gum Ammoniac—*Ferula* spp.
Gum Arabic—*Acacia vera*
Gum Bdellium—*Bursera* spp.
Gum Mastic—*Pistachia lentiscus*
Gum Scammony—*Convolvulus scammonia*
Gum Tragacanth—*Astragalus gummifer*


Hazel—*Corylus* spp.
Heather—*Calluna* spp. or *Erica* spp.
*x* Heliotrope—*Heliotropium europaeum* or *H. arborescens*
*x* Hellebore, Black—*Helleborus niger*
*x* Hemlock—*Conium maculatum*
~ Hemp—*Cannabis sativa*
*x* Henbane—*Hyoscyamus niger*
Hibiscus—*Hibiscus* spp.
Holly—*Ilex aquifolium* or *I. opaca*
Honeysuckle—*Lonicera caprifolium*
~ Hops—*Humulus lupulus*
P Horehound—*Marrubium vulgare*
*x* Hyacinth—*Hyacinthus orientalis*
Hyssop—*Hyssopus officinalis*


Iris—*Iris* spp.
Irish Moss—*Chondrus crispus*
*x* Ivy—*Hedera* spp.


Jasmine—*Jasminum officinale* or *J. odoratissimum*
~P Juniper—*Juniperus communis*

Kava Kava—*Piper methysticum*
Kelp (sea plants including Bladderwrack)—*Fucus visiculosis*
Knotgrass—*Polygonum aviculare*
Lavender—*Lavendula officinale* or *L. vera*
Lemon—*Citrus limon*
Lemon Balm—*Melissa officinalis*
P Lemongrass—*Cymbopogon citratus*
Lemon Verbena—*Lippia citriodora*
~ P Licorice—*Glycyrrhiza glabra*
Lilac—*Syringa vulgaris*
Lily—*Lilium* spp.
Lime—*Citrus limetta*
Lotus—*Nymphaea lotus*
Lovage—*Levisticum officinale*
Lupine—*Lupinus* spp.

~ Mace—*Myristica fragrans*
Magnolia—*Magnolia* spp.
P Maidenhair fern—*Adiantum pedatim*
Mallow—*Malva* spp.
x Mandrake—*Mandragora officinale*
Maple—*Acer* spp.
Marigold—*Calendula officinalis*
Marjoram—*Origanum majorana* or *O. vulgare*
Mastic, Gum—*Pistachia lentiscus*
Meadowsweet—*Spiraea filipendula*
Mimosa—*Acacia dealbata*
Mimulus—*Mimulus moschatus*
Mint—*Mentha spicata* (Spearmint); *M. piperita* (Peppermint)
x Mistletoe, American—*Phoradendron flavescens*
x Mistletoe, European—*Viscum album*
Mormon Tea—*Ephedra* spp.
Moss, Club—*Lycopodium clavatum*
P Mugwort—*Artemisia vulgaris*
Mullein—*Verbascum thapsus*
x Mums—*Chrysanthemum* spp.
Musk Thistle—*Carduus nutans*
Mustard—*Brassica* spp.
P Myrrh—*Comniphora myrrha*
Myrtle—*Myrtus communis*

x  Narcissus—*Narcissus fazetta*
   Neroli (essential oil of the Bitter Orange)—*Citrus aurantium*
   Nettle—*Urtica dioica*
   Niaouli—*Melaleuca viridiflora nigrum*
x  Nightshade—*Solanum*
~  Nutmeg—*Myristica fragrans*

   Oak—*Quercus alba*
   Oakmoss—*Evernia prunastri* or *E. furfuraceae*
   Olive—*Olea europaea*
   Orchid—*Orchis* spp.
P  Opoponax—*Comniphora erythraceae;* var. *glabrescens*
   Orange—*Citrus sinensis*
   Orris—*Iris florentina*
P  Osha—*Ligusticum porteri*

   Palmarosa—*Cymbopogon martini*
   Pansy—*Viola tricolor*
   Parsley—*Petroselinum sativum*
   Passion Flower—*Passiflora incarnata*
   Patchouly—*Pogostemon cablin* or *P. patchouli*
   Peach—*Prunus persica*
P  Pennyroyal—*Mentha pulegium*
   Peony—*Paeonia officinalis*
   Pepper, Black—*Piper nigrum*
   Pepper, Chile—*Capsicum* spp.
   Peppermint—*Mentha piperita*
   Pepperwort—*Lepidium latifolium* or *Polygonum hydropiper?*
~  Periwinkle—*Vinca major*
x  Pine—*Pinus* spp.
   Plumeria—*Plumeria acutifolia*
   Pokeberry—*Phytolacca americana*
   Pomegranate—*Punica granatum*
   Poplar—*Populus tremuloides*
   Poppy—*Papaver* spp.
   Primose—*Primula vulgaris*

x  Ranunculus—*Ranunculus* spp.
~  Red Sandalwood—*Sanicula marilandica*
   Red Storax—*Styrax* spp.

~ P Rhubarb—*Rheum* spp.
　Rose—*Rosa* spp.
　Rose Geranium—*Pelargonium graveolens*
　Rosemary—*Rosmarinus officinalis*
P Rowan—*Sorbus acuparia*
P Rue—*Ruta graveolens*

　Saffron—*Crocus sativus*
　Sagapen—??? (See Spirit Incense #2)
　Sage—*Salvia officinalis*
　Sagebrush—*Artemesia* spp.
　St. John's Wort—*Hypericum perforatum*
~ Sandalwood—*Santalum album*
　Sarsaparilla—*Smilax aspera*
　Sassafras—*Sassafras albidum*
　Selenetrope—??? (See Moon Incense #2)
　Sesame—*Sesamum orientale*
　Solomon's Seal—*Polygonatum officinale* or *P. multiflorum*
　Spearmint—*Mentha spicata*
　Spikenard—*Nardostachys jatamansi*
　Star Anise—*Illicum verum*
~ Stephanotis—*Stephanotis florabunda*
　Storax—*Liquidambar orientalis*
　Strawberry—*Fragaria vesca*
　Sumbul—*Ferula sumbul*
　Sunflower—*Helianthus annuus*
~ Sweet Flag—*Acorus calamus*
　Sweetgrass—*Hierochloe odorata*
　Sweet Pea—*Lathrys odoratus*

　Tamarisk—*Tamarix* spp.
　Tangerine—*Citrus reticulata*
P Tansy—*Tanacetum vulgare*
　*Tapsus barbatus*—Unknown. Perhaps *Taxus baccata* (Yew) faultily
　　transcribed over the centuries. *Barbatus* means "barbed or
　　bearded" but this isn't much of a clue. I truly don't know.
　Tarragon—*Artemesia dracunculus*
　Tea, Black—*Thea sinensis*
　Thistle—*Carduus* spp.
　Thyme—*Thymus vulgaris*

Ti—*Cordyline terminalis*
~ Tobacco—*Nicotiana* spp.
x Tonka—*Dipteryx odorata*
Tragacanth, Gum—*Astragalus gummifer*
x Trefoil—*Trifolium* spp.
Tuberose—*Polianthes tuberosa*

Valerian—*Valeriana officinalis*
Vanilla—*Vanilla aromatica* or *V. planifolia*
Vervain—*Verbena officinalis*
P Vetivert—*Vetiveria zizanioides*
Violet—*Viola odorata*

x Water Parsnip—*Sium latifolium?*
Wheat—*Triticum* spp.
White Willow—*Salix alba*
Wintergreen—*Gaultheria procumbens*
x Wisteria—*Wisteria* spp.
x Wolfsbane—*Aconitum napellus*
Wood Aloe—*Aquilaria agallocha*
Wood Betony—*Betonica officinalis*
~ Woodruff —*Asperula odorata*
x Wormwood—*Artemesia absinthium*

P Yarrow—*Achillea millefolium*
Yellow Daisies—perhaps *Chrysanthemum leucanthemum*
Yerba Santa—*Eriodictyon californicum*
x Yew—*Taxus baccata*
Ylang-Ylang—*Canaga odorata*

# General Index

# ☾ LOOK FOR THE CRESCENT MOON

*Llewellyn publishes hundreds of books on your favorite subjects! To get these exciting books, including the ones on the following pages, check your local bookstore or order them directly from Llewellyn.*

## ORDER BY PHONE

- Call toll-free within the U.S. and Canada, 1-800-THE MOON
- In Minnesota, call (612) 291-1970
- We accept VISA, MasterCard, and American Express

## ORDER BY MAIL

- Send the full price of your order (MN residents add 7% sales tax) in U.S. funds, plus postage & handling to:

  **Llewellyn Worldwide**
  **P.O. Box 64383, Dept. L128-8**
  **St. Paul, MN 55164–0383, U.S.A.**

## POSTAGE & HANDLING

(For the U.S., Canada, and Mexico)

- $4.00 for orders $15.00 and under
- $5.00 for orders over $15.00
- No charge for orders over $100.00

We ship UPS in the continental United States. We ship standard mail to P.O. boxes. Orders shipped to Alaska, Hawaii, The Virgin Islands, and Puerto Rico are sent first-class mail. Orders shipped to Canada and Mexico are sent surface mail.

**International orders:** Airmail—add freight equal to price of each book to the total price of order, plus $5.00 for each non-book item (audio tapes, etc.).

**Surface mail**—Add $1.00 per item.

*Allow 4–6 weeks for delivery on all orders.*
*Postage and handling rates subject to change.*

## DISCOUNTS

We offer a 20% discount to group leaders or agents. You must order a minimum of 5 copies of the same book to get our special quantity price.

## FREE CATALOG

Get a free copy of our color catalog, *New Worlds of Mind and Spirit.* Subscribe for just $10.00 in the United States and Canada ($30.00 overseas, airmail). Many bookstores carry *New Worlds*— ask for it!

**Visit our website at www.llewellyn.com for more information.**

## THE MAGICAL HOUSEHOLD
### Empower Your Home with Love, Protection, Health and Happiness
### Scott Cunningham & David Harrington

Whether your home is a small apartment or a palatial mansion, you want it to be something special. Now it can be with *The Magical Household*. Learn how to make your home more than just a place to live. Turn it into a place of security, life, fun and magic. Here, you will not find the complex magic of the ceremonial magician. Rather, you will learn simple, quick and effective magical spells that use nothing more than common items in your house: furniture, windows, doors, carpet, pets, etc. You will learn to take advantage of the intrinsic power and energy that is already in your home, waiting to be tapped. You will learn to make magic a part of your life. The result is a home that is safeguarded from harm and a place which will bring you happiness, health and more.

**0-87542-124-5, 208 pp., 5¼ x 8, illus., softcover** **$9.95**

## SPELL CRAFTS
### Creating Magical Objects
### Scott Cunningham &
### David Harrington

Since early times, crafts have been intimately
linked with spirituality. When a woman carefully shaped a water jar from the clay she'd
gathered from a river bank, she was performing
a spiritual practice. When crafts were used to
create objects intended for ritual or that sym-
bolized the Divine, the connection between the craftsperson and
divinity grew more intense. Today, handcrafts can still be more
than a pastime—they can be rites of power and honor; a religious
ritual. After all, hands were our first magical tools.

*Spell Crafts* is a modern guide to creating physical objects for the
attainment of specific magical goals. It is far different from magic
books that explain how to use purchased magical tools. You will
learn how to fashion spell brooms, weave wheat, dip candles,
sculpt clay, mix herbs, bead sacred symbols and much more, for a
variety of purposes. Whatever your craft, you will experience the
natural process of moving energy from within yourself (or within
natural objects) to create positive change.

**0-87542-185-7, 224 pp., 5¼ x 8, illus., photos**                    **$10.00**

**EARTH POWER**
**Techniques of Natural Magic**
**Scott Cunningham**

Magick is the art of working with the forces of Nature to bring about necessary and desired changes. The forces of Nature—expressed through Earth, Air, Fire and Water—are our "spiritual ancestors" who paved the way for our emergence from the prehistoric seas of creation. Attuning to and working with these energies in magick not only lends you the power to affect changes in your life, it also allows you to sense your own place in the larger scheme of Nature. Using the "Old Ways" enables you to live a better life and to deepen your understanding of the world. The tools and powers of magick are around you, waiting to be grasped and utilized. This book gives you the means to put Magick into your life, shows you how to make and use the tools, and gives you spells for every purpose

**0-87542-121-0, 176 pp., 5¼ x 8, illus., softcover**                    **$9.95**

## CUNNINGHAM'S ENCYCLOPEDIA OF MAGICAL HERBS
### Scott Cunningham

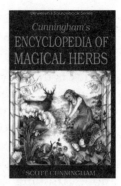

This is the most comprehensive source of herbal data for magical uses ever printed! Almost every one of the over 400 herbs are illustrated, making this a great source for herb identification. For each herb you will also find: magical properties, planetary rulerships, genders, associated deities, folk and Latin names and much more. To make this book even easier to use, it contains a folk name cross reference, and all of the herbs are fully indexed.

There is also a large annotated bibliography, and a list of mail order suppliers so you can find the books and herbs you need. Like all of Cunningham's books, this one does not require you to use complicated rituals or expensive magical paraphernalia. Instead, it shares with you the intrinsic powers of the herbs. Thus, you will be able to discover which herbs, by their very nature, can be used for luck, love, success, money, divination, astral projection, safety, psychic self-defense and much more. Besides being interesting and educational it is also fun, and fully illustrated with unusual woodcuts from old herbals. This book has rapidly become the classic in its field. It enhances books such as 777 and is a must for all Wiccans.

**0-87542-122-9, 336 pp., 6 x 9, illus., softcover** **$14.95**